George W. Pratt

An Account of the British Expedition Above the Highlands of

the Hudson River

George W. Pratt

An Account of the British Expedition Above the Highlands of the Hudson River

ISBN/EAN: 9783337329303

Printed in Europe, USA, Canada, Australia, Japan

Cover: Foto ©Andreas Hilbeck / pixelio.de

More available books at **www.hansebooks.com**

AN ACCOUNT

OF THE

BRITISH EXPEDITION

ABOVE THE

Highlands of the Hudson River,

AND OF

THE EVENTS CONNECTED WITH THE BURNING OF KINGSTON IN 1777.

READ BEFORE

The Ulster Historical Society,

BY

GEORGE W. PRATT

ALBANY:
MUNSELL & ROWLAND, 78 STATE STREET.
1861.

PREFACE.

This paper was prepared for the Annual Meeting of The Ulster Historical Society, held at Stone Ridge on the 18th October, 1860, with no higher aim than to lay before the members, in a connected form, some of the materials of our local history during the period of the Revolution; and to preserve facts yet in the memory of our older inhabitants, before they too should pass into the "land of forgetfulness." It is much to be regretted that an earlier effort, to record the events of the burning of Kingston, by some more familiar hand, has not been made; now the Historical Society will look after the fragments that remain. With my thanks to many friends in the county, as well as in New York and Albany, who have facilitated in various ways the investigation, and this brief apology for the crudeness of my sketch, it is committed to the indulgence of the Society. G. W. PRATT.

ATTWOOD, IN ESOPUS, Nov. 1860.

Eighty-three years ago this day, Thursday, October 16th, 1777, the village of Kingston was burned by the common enemy. The Ulster Historical Society has chosen to keep in remembrance this anniversary in the day of holding its annual meeting.

Notwithstanding the severe blow our forefathers experienced in this event, and the almost universal cry for vengeance which arose throughout the land, it is somewhat surprising that even contemporary accounts should differ as to the exact day of the landing at Esopus. A desire on the part of the Executive Committee of the Society to fix the true date, led me to investigate the subject, and I will therefore at once proceed to mention some of the statements.

Stedman, a British military historian, says the event happened on the *thirteenth* of October, 1777 ;[1] in this he is followed by Gordon, in his *History*,[2] and by Lossing, in his *Field Book of the Revolution*,[3] as well as in a more recent publication. A similar date occurs in an extract from the *New York Packet*,[4] and also in Ramsey's *History of the American Revolution*.

In Beatson's *Naval and Military Memoirs*[5] we have the date of the *fifteenth*, with which a note to Sparks's *Correspondence of the American Revolution* agrees[6], and this is perhaps more generally followed. But Beatson, in a note (p. 249), gives the date of the 16th, which may thus transfer his testimony to the other side ; and a very late work, the *New American Encyclopædia* (*sub voce* Kingston) has it upon the 17th. The British official reports of the expedition are not specific as to the time of the landing. Gen. Vaughan says " on the evening of the 15th instant I arrived off Esopus," and then goes on to detail the events of the action, but so worded as not to be at

---

[1] Vol. 1, p. 365.   [2] Vol. II, p. 579.   [3] Vol. I, p. 388.
[4] In Moore's Diary of the Revolution, I, p. 510.
[5] IV, p. 237.   [6] II p. 14.

I

variance with the evidence to be offered in favor of the date of the 16th. Sir James Wallace gives no time.

The following will fix the true date to be that of the sixteenth

Letter from Governor Clinton to Gen. Gates: Kingston. 16th Oct. 1777, 1 o'clock.—"I am to inform you that the Enemy's Fleet, consisting of upwards of thirty sail, anchored last night about six miles below the Landing Place of the town which they now lie opposite to and appear to be making preparations for landing, &c."

Letter from Gov. Clinton to Gen. Putnam, dated "Marbletown, seven miles from Kingston, 17 October, 1777," * * "Kingston was burnt yesterday afternoon, because I had not troops to defend it." *

Draft of a letter from the Council to the N. Y. Delegates in the Continental Congress:[1] "And on the *sixteenth* instant about two hours before the Governor's troops, who made a forced march could arrive, gained the Landing; and and faintly opposed by about 150 militia only, marched immediately up to Kingston and reduced the whole town to ashes."[2]

A sort of journal of the events of the expedition, printed in Rivington's Gazette of Nov. 3d, 1777, dates the burning on the 16th, and in this differs from the other account in that paper.

The testimony of another eye-witness I am permitted to quote, through the customary courtesy of our respected President; it is taken from a valuable diary which the heads of the well-known family of Hasbrouck have kept for several generations. The entry is in the handwriting of Col. Abraham Hasbrouck, and runs thus:

"1777. Oct. 16. Then the enemy under the command of General Henry Clinton and General Vaughan, came to Kingston, in Esopus, and burnt my dwelling houses, barn, cider house or store house, and another barn, wagon house at my late dwelling house, and also a small out-kitchen which was left standing when my dwelling house was burnt down the 23d of October, 1776, and the enemy burnt all the houses, barns (except one house and barn) in the town, church and county house likewise, laid everything in a rubbish of ashes,

---

[1] Sparks' *Correspondence of the Amer. Revolution*, II, 543.
[2] Jour. Prov. Conv., I, 1072.

fences and everything they came to, and they conveyed with them one negro man named Henry, two negro wenches, Nancy and Flora, and destroyed all my household goods and furniture, and my library of books. My loss I sustained this time, I compute no less than £5000 at least, and house I had in New York burnt by the enemy last year, or in the year 1776. *   *   *
Thanks be to God for his great goodness, I, my wife and children escaped and unhurt out of the enemy's hands. Yet my sons Jacobus, Abraham and Daniel was in the opposing of the enemy from landing and to oppose them to come to Kingston, and showers of shot flew on every side of them.

I pray the Lord will support me under so heavy a trial, and must say with Job, The Lord hath given and the Lord hath taken, the Lord's name may be praised. The Lord is able to restore it again, and much more even an hundred fold. His will be done."   *   *
And after some further pious remarks, concludes, " I write this at my son-in-law's, Abraham Hooghteling, where I am at present, Nov. 10, 1777."

A petition of the trustees of Kingston for the rebuilding of the court-house, dated in 1782, and preserved in the *Legislative papers* in the State Library, and the inscription placed upon the new court-house both mention the day.

If further evidence could be required, it might be added that no difference of opinion, as to the date of the *sixteenth*, has ever existed among the descendants of the villagers of 1777.

The principal events upon the North River which immediately preceded the attack upon Kingston, may not, perhaps, be more precisely stated than by copying the following dispatch, the most of which, appeared in the *London Gazette*, of Dec. 2d, 1777, but the present complete copy, has been recently obtained from the Admiralty, in London.

Dispatch from Commodore Hotham to Vice Admiral, Lord Viscount Howe.

PRESTON, OFF PEEK's HILL CREEK, }
9 Octber, 1777. {

My Lord :
Sir Hy. Clinton having thought it adviseable to make a Diversion at this juncture up the North River,

and the necessary Arrangements being made in Consequence; the Flat Boats and Batteaux on the 3d Inst. proceeded to Spikindevil Creek in Three Divisions under the Captains Pownall, Jordan and Stanhope; Captain Pownall having the direction of the whole.

A body of about 1100 troops were embarked in them that evening, and the same Night proceeded to Tarry Town, where they landed at day-break, and occupied the Heights adjoining. A Second Division, nearly of that number, marched out at the same time from Kingsbridge, and formed a junction by land with those who passed by water. The Squadron under Captain Ommanney had moved up the Day before to receive them, the smaller Part of it, namely, the Galleys and armed Vessels (as they might be to act separately). I thought it adviseable on this Occasion to make a distinct Command, and could not place them better than under the direction of Sir James Wallace, whose knowledge of the River, as well as Captain Ommanney's, we fully experienced the Advantage of.

The Third Division of Troops were embarked in Transports, and on the 4th in the morning, left New York, under Convoy of the Preston, and in the Course of the same Tide, arrived off Tarry Town.

The general Embarkation was that Night made, and the Wind being still favourable the Whole, preceeded by the Squadron under Sir James Wallace as advanced Guard, reached Verplank's Point at Noon the Day following, and those in the Flat Boats landed with Appearance only of an Opposition. Sir James Wallace was immediately dispatched higher up the River to cut off the Enemy's Communication by Peak's Hill Ferry.

The 6th at Day-break the general Debarkation took Place, and all the Troops, except about Four Hundred, who were left to secure Verplank's Neck, were soon landed at Stoney Point, upon the opposite Shore, from whence they had about Twelve Miles to march through a mountainous and rugged Road to Fort Clinton and Montgomery.

The Ships and Transports then moved higher up and anchored opposite Peak's Hill Landing.

In the Afternoon the advanced Squadron and the two Frigates got under sail and opened Fort Montgomery, with a view only to make an Appearance, and thereby to cause a Diversion in favour of the Attack, which we observed had now begun. Sir James by the Help of his Oars, got near enough in with 2 Gallies to throw some shot into the Fort. The Cannonading and Fire of Musquetry continued until Night, when, by a most spirited Exertion a general and vigorous Assault was made, and the Two important Forts of Clinton and Montgomery, fell by Storm to his Majesty's Arms. On which I have the Honour to congratulate your Lordship most sincerely. The Rebel Frigates are both Burnt, with a Galley, and a Sloop of Ten Guns is taken.

The loss on the Enemy's Side is not yet exactly known, but they are supposed to have had about 100 killed and 250 taken Prisoners. The greatest Loss on the Side of the King's Troops are about 40 killed, among whom are some valuable Officers, namely, Lieutenant Colonel Campbell, Major Sill, Major Grant and Capt. Stewart, and about 150 wounded.

A Summons signed by Sir Henry Clinton and myself was the next Day sent up to Fort Constitution, by a Flag of Truce, which being fired at returned, and determined the General immediately to correct the Insult by an Attack. An Embarkation was accordingly made on the Morning of the 8th, and proceeded up the river for that Purpose, under cover of the Galleys.

We found upon our Arrival the Fort had been abandoned in great Confusion, their Barracks burnt, but all their Artillery left The whole Number of Cannon taken in the Three Forts amount to 67, with a large Quantity of Provisions, Ammunition and Stores of all kinds to a very considerable Amount. I have directed such part of the Chain and Boom as cannot be saved to be destroyed; the Construction of both give strong Proofs of Labour, Industry and Skill.

Sir James Wallace with his flying Squadron is gone still higher up the River, and if he passes the Chevaux de Frize at Polipous Island, he may do essential service, as there can be nothing to give him any Interruption.

When it is considered that this Attack was made after a most fatiguing March over Precipices and thro' Roads almost impenetrable, which made it impossible for the Troops to avail themselves of the use of the Cannon so necessary for such a Purpose, and the little Assistance they could therein promise themselves from the Ships; the Access from the Highlands to the Forts, rendering the Approach to them so precarious, it redounds the more to the Credit of an Enterprise, which was formed and executed with equal Judgment, Valour and Success.

The Captains, Officers, and Men under my Command have been so strenuously zealous in their Exertions on this Occasion, that every testimony is due from me in appreciation of their conduct during this service of fatigue, of which Captain Pownall has had his share, and is well able to inform your Lordship of every particular.

Since I had the honor of writing to your Lordship by the Zebra, the Unicorn, Galatea, Danae and Cerberus arrived, but all of them are in great (*want of*) repairs and stores. The fifty gun ship's people, having been employed in the Flat Boats, will account to your Lordship for their not having joined you so soon as you might have expected; but if the General remains any time, I shall relieve the Bristol's Flat Boat even by some of the Frigate's, that she may be at liberty to proceed with the next Express. I have directed Captain Onslow to carry on the current date at York until my return, and am to acquaint you that I have appointed Mr. George Stevens Surgeon's Second Mate of the Preston to act as Surgeon of the Elephant, till your Lordship's pleasure be known   I have, &c.,
                                         W. HOTHAM.

P. S. I have the further pleasure to acquaint your Lordship that General Tryon is just returned from Continental Village, where he has destroyed barracks for 1500 men, with stores to a considerable amount.

The capture of Forts Clinton and Montgomery and the abandonment of the other posts, enabled the British to destroy the boom and chain which had been extended across the river from Constitution island to West Point; and also make a passage for their vessels through the chevaux-de-frize at Pollopel's island above. These impediments had cost the Americans much trouble and expense, and a particular account of them will be found in Ruttenber's *Obstructions to the Navigation of Hudson's River*, not long since issued in Munsell's elegant Historical Series.

Sir Henry Clinton determined to make a still further

diversion in favor of Burgoyne, or we might rather say, to start an expedition to punish the people upon the banks of the Hudson for their want of loyalty, at the same time secure some prize money and general booty. Accordingly he organized what is known as the *second expedition under Gen. Vaughan.* Stedman assures us that the necessity of a diversion in favor of Burgoyne was not even suspected. Preparatory to this expedition he had however dispatched Captain Sir James Wallace[1] with a galley, a schooner and three other small vessels to reconnoitre the river. They left the Highlands on the 11th, and penetrated to within three miles of Pough-keepsie, and returned in safety, having "burnt Van Keuren's Mills and several buildings on the other side of the river with several old vessels along shore."[2]

The report of Sir James determined the movement, and the following among other naval vessels were placed under his command, viz: *Diligent,* Lieut. Farn-ham ; *Dependence,* Lieut. Clarke ; *Spitfire,* Lieut. Scott ; *Crane,* Master Hitchcock ; *Raven,* 14 guns, Capt. Stan-hope. Capt. Wallace himself sailed in the armed vessel the *Friendship,* 22 guns, Capt. A. Jas. Pye Molloy. To the armed vessels were added about twenty galleys and flat boats, manned from the crew of the Bristol, Experi-ment, and other large frigates lying below, the latter being under the subordinate command of Capt. Stanhope. In order to secure the communication, the *Mercury* of 20 guns, was stationed at Pollopel's island ; the *Cerberus,* 28, at Stony Point ; the *Tartar,* 28, at Fort Clinton ; Commodore Hotham's own ship, the *Preston,* 50 guns, anchoring between these two last and within signalling distance of either.

On these vessels, about 1600 men[3] under the com-mand of Major Gen. the Hon. John Vaughan embarked.[4] It consisted of the 7th (Royal Fusileers), 26th and 63d Regiments.[5] It has been often stated that the British force was about 3600 men, but it is evident, from a field return of the forces serving under Sir Wm. Howe, made

[1] Sir James Wallace. (Note I.)
[2] Zeph Platt to the Council of Safety, dated Poughkeepsie Oct. 12th (*Gates Papers*).
[3] Commodore Hotham's letter to Lord Howe, dated "Preston, off Peek's Kiln Creek, 15th Oct., 1777."
[4] Gen. Vaughan. (Note II.)
[5] The same to the same, dated "St. Albans, New York, 21st Oct., 1777."

Nov. 1st, 1777, a copy of which, obtained from the War Office in London, is in the writer's possession, that the strength of the land forces could not have exceeded sixteen hundred men The total quota of these three regiments being 1530, while the actual effective "present" on the first of November was only 1261, and they had no detachments out. Sir Henry Clinton states his force at the storming of the forts to have been 3000 men, from which the mistake of the number on Vaughan's second expedition has no doubt arisen.

The 7th Regiment was commanded by Lieut. Col. Clarke, its nominal Colonel, the overbearing General Prescott, being actually a prisoner to the Americans, thanks to the intrepidity of William Barton, whose exploit in seizing him in his bed at Newport, will not soon fade from the annals of heroism. This regiment lost its colors, which had been left in store, by the capture of Fort Chamblée, in October, 1775, during Montgomery's invasion of Canada. Lord Adam Gordon's Regiment, the 26th, was in the field under its Major, also named Gordon. To this regiment belonged the unfortunate André, who although a captain in the line, was temporarily on the staff of Major Gen. Grey, and therefore not present at the burning of Kingston. The 63d (Gen. Grant's) had suffered severely in the attack on the Highland forts, and where its commandant, Major Sill, was killed ; several of its officers did not accompany the expedition, and although the strongest in numbers, was on this occasion, probably commanded by Captain Hazlewood. Captain Lord Rawdon, better known at a later period of the war, was absent from his regiment at this time.

The expedition sailed from Peekskill on the 14th of October, with a fair wind, and the following night anchored off Esopus island. They did not stop much along the way, occasionally capturing a vessel, and now and then firing at the dwelling of some well known Whig, like that of Henry Livingston, at the lower landing in Poughkeepsie, where we are told by Mr. Lossing, in his interesting *Field Book of the Revolution*, the marks of a shot may still be seen.

The Americans were not idle or listless at this time : Governor Clinton who barely escaped capture at the storming of the forts, on the 7th, from New Windsor, communicated the loss of these places to the Legislature then in session at Kingston, with a request for them to urge the detachment of the Ulster and Dutchess militia from the northern army under Gen. Gates. Rightly judging that the enemy would endeavor to penetrate farther than the Highlands, he had thus reason to fear that they would attempt Kingston, the most important town on the river between New York and Albany, and on the 10th he thus writes to the Council :

HEAD QUARTERS, Mrs. Falls, 10 Oct., 1777.

Gentlemen :

When I wrote you last, I was in great hopes of being able to have collected and embodied as many of the Militia of this and Orange County as with the two small Continental Regiments now with me, and the Reinforcement promised me by General I. Putnam, I should have such a formidable force as to enable me to prevent the enemy's penetrating the country, by throwing myself in between them and the most important places as they moved up the River. But I am sorry to inform you I am greatly disappointed in my expectations. The Militia do not join me as I could wish, they are well disposed but anxious about the immediate safety of their respective families, who for many miles back are moving yet farther from the River, many of them come in in the morning, return in the evening, and I never know when I have them or what my strength is. The Reinforcement I had reason to expect and was promised by General Putnam, I am informed by a letter from him last night is only to consist of Brinker-hoof's Regiment, which I am sure will not pass the river, indeed it would be unreasonable to expect them. This being my situation I think it my duty to advise you of it, as my only hopes are that my force may not be known to the enemy and that this may deter them from doing what if they should attempt, I could not prevent.

I have 7 Field Pieces with me, five of the heaviest I have ordered on the west side of the Wallkill, towards Shawangunk, which is the route I mean to take to Kingston, the moment the enemy move up the River.

I wish some small works could be thrown up towards the Esopus Landing so as to cover the Landing and the Defiles leading to the Town. Every man that can fire a Gun should be immediately embodied and employed at

2

those works. I rejoice with you on the most agreeable Intelligence from the Northward, and thank you for the Early Communication of it. I know of no Enemy on this side Butterhill Clove. The four Vessels that were near Polopels Island fell down out of sight yesterday Evening.   I am with much Esteem,

Your most obedt. servt.,

GEO. CLINTON.

The regiments of militia from the lower part of Ulster county suffered considerably in killed, wounded and prisoners at the forts, so that it was no easy matter for Governor Clinton to collect a sufficient force to resist the threatened demonstration. On the east bank General Putnam had about six thousand men, mostly militia, and this army now held Sir Henry Clinton in check in this direction, although it is not quite so clear that Gen. Putnam could not have rendered a more important service in going to the assistance of the garrison of the Highland forts on the 6th. At any rate the royal generals did not seem to be in much fear of this army. Perhaps a critical narrative of the events in the Highlands during these few days, in which the matter will appear in its true light, may yet be written.

Governor Clinton says his plan, in case of the advance of the enemy, would be to make a forced march down the west side of the Waalkill and thus cover Kingston.

The capture of a spy by the name of Daniel Taylor, charged with a message from Sir Henry Clinton to General Burgoyne occurred on the 9th; the incidents of this man's arrest, trial and execution I have thrown together in the appendix.[1]

Sir James Wallace's reconnoitering expedition up the river on the 11th, alarmed the Governor, and from "Little Britain, 3 miles from New Windsor, 12th Oct., 1777," after some general matters he writes to the council at Kingston, as follows:

"I am at this moment favoured with your letter of yesterday. The militia of Shawangunk are now with me. I have sent a proper guard there from another quarter, for the artillery; which, in my opinion, is much better than to leave men of the neighbourhood for that purpose. Col. Snyder's regiment may continue at

---

[1] Note III.

Kingston, to throw up the necessary works to defend the landing and town. The rest of the reinforcement from the northward must immediately join me. Were the whole to continue with you, they would not be able to meet the enemy should they pass by and land near Kingston ; and should they take their route by land, which is most likely, with my present force, which consists of the militia of this quarter of the country, two small continental regiments and Col. Sutherland's regiment consisting of 130 men. Out of these I have strong guards along the river shore who have orders to keep pace with the vessels now in the river, and throw themselves between them and Kingston landing, should they go that high up. I am persuaded it is not only for the safety of Kingston, which I have much at heart, but for that of the country in general, that I should have my whole force collected to one point ; as in that case I shall be able to meet and oppose the progress of the enemy, or at least throw myself in between the enemy, and such places as may be an object with them to gain, which shall be my constant care to do."

The postscript adds, "From many circumstances, I am persuaded the enemy are about moving. Gen. Clinton's being out when my flag was down yesterday, this small fleet coming up the river confirms me in this opinion ; and I believe it will be by land, against some of our stores, and to ravage the country." [1]

By a resolution of the Convention passed December 21st, 1775, the Ulster County Jail was made the jail of Congress.[2] Johannes Sleght, Chairman of the Kingston Committee, in a letter written on the 8th of July, 1776, tells the Provincial Congress that " it is also well known that our town has for a long time been crowded (and is yet) with a set of ministerial cut-throats, regular officers and soldiers sent here as prisoners." [3]

These prisoners, Gov. Clinton directs the Commissary, Abram B. Bancker,[4] to remove to Wawarsing ; and as there could be no doubt of the benevolent intentions of Sir Henry Clinton towards the rebel authorities and their estates, he forwarded his personal effects from his

---

[1] Jour. Prov. Conv., I, p. 1069.
[2] Jour. Prov. Conv., I, p. 231. [3] *Ibid.* II, p. 305.
[4] Mr. Bancker was, for many years after the revolution, Clerk of the Senate, and died at Kingston, Feb. 7th, 1806, aged 51 years.

house in Little Britain to Kingston—his brother-in-law, Doctor Peter Tappen, removing Mrs. Clinton and the family to Pleasant Valley, in Dutchess County, where they remained until the marauders returned to New York.

A statement of the plan of government of the State, and the action upon it down to this period, will enable us to appreciate the position of affairs at this juncture.

The revolutionary authority in New York was exercised by a Provincial Convention which assembled at the Exchange in New York city, April 20th, 1775, and to which Charles DeWitt, George Clinton and Levi Pawling were sent as delegates from Ulster County.

The members from this county in the subsequent Provincial Congress were as follows :

First Provincial Congress.

Met at New York, May 23d, 1775.

Col. Johannes Hardenbergh of Rosendale, Col. James Clinton of New Windsor, Egbert Dumond of Kingston, Charles Clinton of Little Britain (not present), Christopher Tappen of Kingston, John Nicholson of New Windsor, and Jacob Hoornbeck of Rochester.

Second Provincial Congress.

Met at New York, Nov. 14th, 1775.

Henry Wisner, Jr., of Walkill, Matthew Rea of Shawangunk, Dirck Wynkoop, Jr., of Kingston, Matthew Cantine of Marbletown, Andries Dewitt of Kingston, Andries Lefever of New Paltz, Thomas Palmer of Newburgh, and Samuel Brewster of New Windsor.

Third Provincial Congress.

Met at at New York, May 14th, 1776.

Col. Charles DeWitt of Hurley. Col. Abraham Hasbrouck of Kingston, Col. Johannes Snyder of Kingston, Matthew Cantine, Matthew Rea, Major Arthur Parks of Montgomery, Henry Wisner, Jr., of Walkill, and Samuel Brewster.

In a list given at the end of the Journal of this Congress the name of George Clinton occurs, and it is noted that he " is now in his place." His name, however, is not included in the published credentials, and he was at that moment a member of the Continental Congress.

The fourth Provincial Congress assembled at White Plains, in Westchester county, July 9th, 1776, when the Declaration of Independence was immediately adopted, and the following day the style of the House was changed to that of the "Convention of the Representatives of the State of New York."

Matthew Cantine, Col. Charles DeWitt, Major Arthur Parks, Col. Levi Pawling, Mathew Rea, Major Christopher Tappen, Col. Johannes Hardenbergh and Henry Wisner, Jr., were the representatives from Ulster County in this body. It adjourned to Fishkill August 29th, 1776—thence it moved to Kingston on the 19th of February, 1777. During this period the government was often in the hands of a small portion of the Convention styled a *Committee of Safety*, so that public affairs could be carried on, it having been found extremely difficult to keep so large a body together at this critical period of our history.

Some sketches of the personal history of the Ulster County Members of these Congresses are included in the appendix.[1]

During this time the local organization was maintained and the friends of liberty were active at home.

A letter from Robert Boyd, Jr., Chairman of the Ulster County Committee, in June, 1776,[2] shows the plan of the county organization :

"The County Committee is composed of two members from each Precinct Committee, save Kingston, which claims the privilege of sending four. The members of the Precinct Committees generally attend County Committee by rotation for their own ease and convenience."

It is very doubtful whether the minutes of the proceedings of either the County or Precinct Committees still exist ; they would be valuable for our local history, and further search for them should be made.

On the 31st of Jan., 1777, it appears that " Messrs. Duane and Robert Yates, returned from Kingston, reported in substance that they had conferred with the

---

[1] Note IV.   [2] Amer. Archives, 4th Series, VI, p. 898.

committee of Kingston, in Ulster county, and find that if the convention should move to that place, fifty members may obtain good accommodations. That the price will be twenty shillings per week. That the Court House or a large room in the said building, will be convenient for the Convention to meet in."[1]

It is thus probable that the Convention, or rather the Committee of Safety, first met at the Court House in Kingston.

The Convention may have changed its place of meeting for a time in consequence of the annoyances arising from the crowded state of the jail below the chamber in the Court House. Indeed, we find that on motion of Governeur Morris, on the 18th of March, 1777, the following curious preamble and resolution was passed.

"Whereas from the past want of care of the prisoners now confined in the jail immediately underneath the Convention Chamber, the same is supposed to have become unwholesome, and very nauseous and disagreeable effluvia arises, which may endanger the health of the members of this Convention. Therefore,

Resolved. That for the preservation of their health, the members of this Convention be at liberty at their pleasure to smoke in the Convention Chamber while the house is sitting and proceeding on business.[2]

Suprising to relate, this smoking resolution met with great opposition among a community of Dutchmen, and it only passed by a majority of three votes, the representatives of two counties not having been able to agree upon this momentous question. No such dispute arose in the Council of New Amsterdam, in the days of Peter "the Headstrong," and it is evident that the elements were much disturbed in these latter days. A horrible account of the condition of the jail in Kingston in April, 1776, is given in a letter of Bryan Leffertse, a state prisoner there, preserved in the Mercantile Library, New York.

I have been somewhat minute in this particular, because it is the general belief, and well founded too, I think, that the Constitution was adopted at the inn of Capt. Evert Bogardus, the rebuilt edifice being afterwards known as the "Constitution House,"—a stone

---

[1] Jour. Prov. Conv., I, p. 794.
[2] Jour. Prov. Conv., I, p. 842.

building standing on the corner of Maiden Lane and Fair street. In the year 1856, having became much dilapidated it was demolished to make way for the residence of James W. Baldwin, Esq., its owner.[1]

After much discussion the Convention adopted the State Constitution on the evening of Sunday, the 20th of April, 1777, and pursuant to a resolution it was proclaimed at the Court House at eleven o'clock on the morning of the 22d following, and on the 13th of May this distinguished body finally dissolved, leaving power in the hands of a Council of Safety.

The election under the Constitution was held,[2] and on the 30th of July the Council declared George Clinton duly chosen Governor ; a copy of the proclamation issued on that occasion has been printed in our *Collections* (vol. I, p. 66).

On the same day it was

" *Ordered*, That the said proclamation be made and published by the Sheriff of Ulster County, at or near the Court House in Kingston, Ulster County, at six o'clock this afternoon.

And in order that due ceremony should be observed in this matter they further

" *Resolved, and Ordered*, That Captain Evert Bogardus and Captain John Elmendorph do cause the companies of militia, under their respective commands, to appear at the Court House in Kingston at six o'clock this afternoon, properly armed and accoutred, at which time and place His Excellency George Clinton will be proclaimed Governor of this State."[3]

The record assures us that it was done in due form in the presence of the Council, and thus was inaugurated the first republican government of the now " Empire State." It was a great day for Kingston, but

---

[1] A woodcut of this building is given in *Barber & Howe's Histor. Collections of N. Y.*, p. 558. Another and more artistic one may be found in Lossing's *Field Book of the Revolution*, vol. I, p. 357, but these authors are in error when they state it to be the identical building in which the Constitution was formed. The stone walls of the original structure undoubtedly remained after the conflagration of the village, but all that fire would consume of it was destroyed by Vaughan. As will afterwards appear, only the house in Wall street now belonging to Abraham T. Van Steenbergh escaped the fire of 1777.

[2] "In the county of Ulster, at the Court House in the town of Kingston; at the house of Ann DuBois, in New Paltz ; at the house of Sarah Hill, in Hanover precinct; at the house of Martin Wygant, in the precinct of Newburgh " (Jour. Prov. Conv., I, p. 917).

[3] Jour. Prov. Conv., I, p. 1022.

the people of this devoted town not long after expiated, " in dust and ashes," their attachment to the principles of liberty, and the peculiar distinction their village enjoyed as the seat of the new State government.

The newly chosen Legislature was appointed to meet at Kingston on the 1st of August, but for weighty reasons Gov. Clinton prorogued it to the 20th of August, and again until Sept. 1st ; however, no quorum of the Senate appeared until the 9th of that month, and the Assembly did not organize until the following day.

At this first Legislature, Col. Levi Pawling of Marbletown attended as the Senator from the Ulster County portion of the middle district ; and John Cantine of Marbletown,[1] Johannes G. Hardenbergh of Rochester, Mathew Rea of Shawangunk, Cornelius C. Schoonmaker of Shawangunk, Col. Johannes Snyder of Kingston,[2] and Henry Wisner, Jr., of Wallkill, were the members of Assembly from Ulster County—then comprehending all the river shore from Murderer's creek near the Highlands to the Sawyer's creek, just above Saugerties, and embracing the present county of Sullivan, with Delaware up to the east branch of the Deleware river, and the north eastern towns of Orange.

The Senate sat at the house of Abraham Van Gaasbeck, a stone building, constructed after the then " Esopus fashion," the last one on the west side of East Front street, near the junction of that street with North Front. This fact is shown by an entry in the Journal of the Provincial Convention,[3] its own records not mentioning any room. This house has recently been occupied by the Rev. Dr. Westbrook.

---

[1] In " *The Indians ; or Narratives of Massacres and Depredations on the Frontier, in Warwasink and its Vicinity, &c.,*" Rondout, 1846, there are some statements not very flattering to the courage of Col. John Cantine.

[2] Johannes Snyder was a Major in the Militia in 1775, but was afterwards appointed to the command of one of the regiments. He resided at Kingston and was one of the superior officers present on the day of the British attack. He seems to have been a Magistrate and Trustee of the Corporation. The present residence of Jonathan H. Hasbrouck, Esq., on the southwest corner of Fair street and Maiden lane, opposite the " Constitution House," occupies the site of his house. I believe that none of his descendants remain at Kingston.

[3] Vol. I, p. 1101. I have the locality of this house from Major Van Gaasbeck, to whom I am much indebted for information relative to the history of Ulster County. This Abraham Van Gaasbeck was a grandson of the worthy Dominie Laurentius Van Gaasbeck, whose diploma (*Med. Doctor*) from the University of Leyden the Major still preserves.

A room in Capt. Bogardus' inn was called the "Assembly Chamber," and the lower house probably held its session there, as they are summoned to meet the Governor and Senate at the Court House, which would hardly have been necessary, had the sessions of the Assembly usually taken place in that building. Besides this, the Supreme Court was organized by Chief Justice Jay, at the Court House, on the ninth of September, and, of course, required the court room for its legitimate purpose.

The Governor resided, during his stay in Kingston, at the house of his brother in-law, Christopher Tappen, Esq., situated on the southwest corner of Wall and North Front streets. It was immediately rebuilt after the fire, and of late has been occupied as a drug store by Peter E. Jansen. At this house Gov. Clinton received the address of the Legislature.

The Legislature remained in session at Kingston until October 7th, when the Senate adjourned for the day, but in fact " without day," the journal of its next meeting, at Poughkeepsie under the head of January 5th, 1778, containing the following :

" About noon on Tuesday the seventh day of October, last, news came by Express of the Reduction of Fort *Montgomery*, in the Highlands, and its Dependencies by the Enemy. And although this Senate therefore adjourned till Wednesday morning, the eighth of October last, yet so many members of the Honorable, the House of Assembly, absented themselves on military Service, and for the necessary care of their Families, in Consequence of the Event, that there was not a sufficient Number of them left at Kingston to form a House for Business ; which rendered the Meeting of the Senate, according to Adjournment, useless ; and therefore the Senate ceased to attend on the public Business, until His Ex., the Gov., thought proper to convene the Legislature of this State, by His Proc. in the Words following, to-wit : &c "[1]

A similar entry occurs in the Assembly Journal, the first part of which document had hardly been completed at Holt's press in Kingston, when Vaughan's expedition landed.

It being impossible to continue Legislative business in the prescribed form, on the seventh of October, a

---

[1] Senate Journal, 1st Session.

meeting of the members of the Senate and Assembly was convened by unanimous consent in Kingston. Senator Pawling and Messrs. Hardenbergh, Snyder, Schoonmaker and Rea, Assemblymen from Ulster County, were in attendance, with about forty other members of the Legislature.

Lieut. Governor Van Courtlandt, was chosen president of the Convention, and John McKesson and Robert Benson, Secretaries.

They remained in session but a few hours, but in order to keep up the local organizations, passed resolutions continuing the county and district committees, as well as the commissioners for detecting and defeating conspiracies, as they existed on the preceding 13th of September.

To defeat the possible intention of the enemy, who was now in possession of the Highlands, should he move up by water, they

" *Resolved,* That the members of the several Committees be, and they hereby are, required to lade all vessels which may be at the different landings, and other places along Hudson's river, with flour, wheat, and any other kind of provisions which may be near the shores of the said river, and send the said sloops and vessels to Albany, &c.

Resolved, That the said committees respectively do forthwith cause all the cattle and live stock near or contiguous to either side of Hudson's River, except such parts thereof as, in their judgment, shall be necessary for the present use of the respective proprietors thereof, to be removed into the interior parts of the country on the several sides of the said river, to be taken care of by keepers to be by them severally appointed.   *   *   *   *   *   And in case any person or persons shall obstinately refuse to permit his, her or their cattle or other stock to be so removed, that then and in such case, the said committee be, and they hereby are empowered to destroy the same, &c., &c."

They then appoint a committee of safety in these terms :

" *Resolved,* That William Floyd, John Morin Scott, Abraham Yates, Johannes Snyder, Egbert Benson, Robert Harper, Peter Pra Van Zandt, Levi Paulding, Daniel Dunscomb, Evert Bancker, Alexander Webster, William B. Whiting and Jonathan Langdon, Esquires,

or any seven of them, be, and they are hereby appointed
a Council of Safety, and they be, and hereby are,
in the recess of the House, vested with the like powers
and authorities which were given to the late Council of
Safety, appointed by the last Convention of this State ;
that every member of the Senate and Assembly, and the
Delegates of this State in Congress, be entitled from time
to time to sit and vote in the said Council ; and that the
said persons, or any seven of them, be and continue a
Council of Safety, so long as the necessities of this
State shall require, and no longer.

Resolved, That the Governor, or in his absence, the
President of the Senate, when they shall respectively
be present at the said Council, shall preside at, and upon
an equal division, have a casting voice in the same."[1]

On the morning of the 8th of October, the new
Council of Safety assembled, and chose Mr. Floyd President *pro tempore.*

In order to secure the state prisoners, a large
number of whom were confined in Kingston jail, as well
as on board two or three vessels moored at the mouth
of the creek, and termed the *Fleet Prison,* the Council
directed them to be removed to Hartford, Conn. Cornelius C. Elmendorph was the Commissary for supplying
these prisoners, and Doctor Luke Kiersted the attending physician. They seem to have been guarded by a
company from Col. Pawling's regiment of militia,
under the command of Capt. Frederick Schoonmaker,
and the armed sloop Hudson, Capt. Benson, was anchored near the prison vessels.

The correspondence between the Council of Safety
and Governor Clinton was actively kept up, men from
Capt. Silvester Salisbury's troop of Kingston Light-
Horse,[2] being stationed on the road south of the village
to facilitate the matter.

The danger from the enemy seemed so imminent
that the public records were ordered boxed and ready
to be moved at a moment's warning : and it was

"*Resolved,* That Messrs. Snyder, Schoonmaker, Langdon and Benson,[3] be requested to take four hundred

---

[1] Jour. Prov. Conv. I, p 1061.

[2] Capt. Salisbury resided in the Pine Bush district of Kingston, and
was connected with the Van Gaasbecks; from their manuscript genealogy
the whole family can be traced out. He died April 10th, 1785, aged 42
or 43 years.

[3] Chancellor Kent's sketch of the life and services of Egbert Benson
may be found in Thompson's *Long Island,* II, p. 487.

pounds, at interest, at six per cent, from Abraham Hasbrouck, Esq.,[1] and pay the same to the Commissioners for conspiracies; and that this Council will indemnify them for the same.[2]"

On the 9th strong resolutions were passed to impress wheat for the use of the troops, and steps taken to secure the military stores Gov. Clinton in a letter read at the afternoon session gives an account of matters after the fall of the forts, and says:

"As soon as ever I find the shipping are likely to pass the chevaux-de-frise, I will by a forced march endeavor to gain Kingston and cover that town. I shall have one brass twenty-four pounder, and six smaller field pieces, which will make a formidable train.

I am persuaded if the militia will join me (which I have reason to hope), we can save the country (a few scattering houses along the river excepted), from destruction, and defeat the enemy's design in assisting their northern army."

The session of the 10th of October is an active one and shows the state of alarm prevailing at Kingston.

A large quantity of saltpetre at the landing is ordered to be removed from the shore, and the Council passed the following resolution:

"*Resolved*, That Colonels Pawling and Snyder be requested to issue the necessary orders to have all the male inhabitants in the districts of their respective regiments of 16 years and upwards capable of bearing arms immediately equipped and provided with arms and ammunition and to appoint proper alarm Posts and places of rendezvous for the respective companies to repair to in case of the approach of the enemy."

Other resolutions direct Gerard Bancker, Vice Treasurer; John Henry, Commissary of Clothing; the Secretaries of the Convention, as well as Messrs. Abram Hasbrouck, Joseph Gasherie,[3] Dirck Wynkoop,

---

[1] Abraham Hasbrouck, Note V.
[2] Jour. Prov. Conv., I, p. 1064.
[3] Joseph Gasherie was appointed, March 13th, 1778, the first Surrogate under the new State Government, and continued in this office until elected Senator from the middle district, in 1784; during his term he was a member of the Council. Immediately after its close he was reappointed Surrogate by Governor Clinton, and held it at the time of his death, which occurred in Kingston, Jan. 16th, 1806.

Jr.,' Christopher Tappen and Samuel Bayard, Jr., who had charge of the Public Records of the Colony (deposited at Kingston in June, 1776), to remove the property in their custody to Rochester. The arrangement for proper places of deposit at Rochester is to be left to Hendricus Hornbeck, Johannes G. Hardenbergh and Comfort Sands.[2] In case of necessity Judge Wynkoop and Oke Sudam will impress teams to convey this property. A captain's guard was afterwards ordered to be furnished from Col. Pawling's regiment for the public records at Rochester.

Kingston seems to have been a general place of deposit for the Westchester, Albany and Ulster County records, which, with the papers of the Receiver General of the Colony, are dispatched to Rochester along with the others.

On the 11th the Council ordered the militia from the vicinity of Shawangunk to join the Governor's army, and all the rest of the Ulster County force to assemble at Kingston. The order to Capt. Benson to land his arms and munitions of war and take provisions to Albany, saved the sloop Hudson from the fate of the other vessels lying off the point.

Where the sessions of the Council had been, up to this time, is not stated in the Journal, but most likely at the Court House. This afternoon the adjournment is to Conrad C. Elmendorf's tavern,[3] where they continued to be held while Kingston remained standing.

The old remark that " there are no Sundays in war " applies to the affairs of State at this juncture, for the Council remained in session all day on Sunday. On the following morning they have Governor Clinton's

[1] A short notice of the public services of Judge Wynkoop is found at p. 69 of vol. I of the Ulster Historical Society's COLLECTIONS. It is to be regretted that the papers of this gentleman have been destroyed ; they might have been of much use in illustrating our local history

[2] For a biographical sketch of Comfort Sands, see Thompson's *History of Long Island*, I, 465.

[3] The inn of Conrad C. Elmendorf was on the northeast corner of Maiden lane and Fair street, and the present house belongs to the family of the late Judge Van Buren. It became somewhat famous as the head quarters of the Clinton party—the " Constitution House," on the other corner, diagonally, being the place of rendezvous for the supporters of Mr. Jay. The older inhabitants of Kingston are wont to repeat some very amusing anecdotes of the warmth of party spirit in those days, while the minutes of the worshipful Trustees of the old Kingston Corporation show that the inns of Bogardus and Elmendorf were rival shrines—the resorts of the Capulets and Montagues of Esopus.

letter of the 11th, dated at "Mrs. Fall's,"[1] in which he graphically describes the purgation of Daniel Taylor, the spy—a letter I reserve for another place. The afternoon session is confined to the business of examining the case of that troublesome old tory, Cadwallader Colden, who is finally allowed to go with his son; Angus McDonald, a prisoner of war, is sent to Hurley on parole, but Roelif Eltinge they commit to jail "until further orders."

The news of the recounoissance of Sir James Wallace towards Poughkeepsie reaches the Council by express from the Governor, on Tuesday morning. The Governor complains of the want of fixed ammunition, which will probably account for the little damage done to the British squadron, which succeeded these vessels. The *Lady Washington* galley, Captain Cook, moved up in advance of the enemy to an anchorage in the Rondout Creek. The Council send Capt. Salisbury's troop down to New Windsor, mainly to serve as expresses. The attendance of the members at these latter sessions is small, but Lieut. Governor Van Courtlandt is always in the chair.

The GATES PAPERS, in the library of the New York Historical Society, supply the last letter Governor Clinton writes to the Council, before setting out for the defence of Esopus.

HEADQUARTERS, NEAR NEW WINDSOR, }
15th Oct., 1777, 9 o'clock, A. M. }

Dear Sir:

I am this moment informed by a light horseman from my guard at New Windsor, that twenty sail of the enemy's shipping (two of them large vessels) are in the river below Butter Hill. There was a heavy fogg on the river in the morning when they were discovered, so that the officer of the guard could not be particular as the size of the vessels; he thinks it highly probable that more may be near at hand and might be seen were it not for the fogg. Had it not been for this movement of the enemy, I intended this day or to-morrow to have drawn my few troops from this place towards the rear of fort Montgomery but I must now desist and watch their motions; and should they land and march against

---

[1] Mrs. Alexander Falls resided at the *Square*, about 4 miles west of the village of New Windsor. The house was occupied in 1850 by Samuel Moore. Lossing's *Field Book*; Eager's *Hist. of Orange Co*, p 640.

me with any considerable force, I shall be constrained
with my present numbers to retreat before them, annoy-
ing them only if favorable opportunities shall offer. I
was in hopes ere now to have received the reinforcement from the northward which you mentioned ; not
a man of which are yet arrived. I wish Col. Pawling
with his regiment was with me. Since writing the
above, the enemy's fleet consisting of 30 sail have
passed Newburg with crowded sail and fair wind are
moving quick up the river ; the front of them are already at the Dans Caamer. There are eight large, square
rigged vessels among them, and all appear to have
troops on board. My troops are parading to march for
Kingston. Our route will be through Shawangunk to
prevent delay in crossing the Paltz River.—I leave
Collo. Woodhull's, McClaughry's and part of Haas-
brouck's regiments as a guard along the river.—Ha-
thorn's is gone to the southward to guard a quantity of
arms towards head-quarters. When he returns he is to
join this guard. I have neither time to copy or read
this scrall ; the substance must be communicated to
Gen. Gates. Let the militia be drawn out ready to
oppose the enemy. I will be with you if nothing extra
happens, before day ; though my troops cannot.

I am, yours &c.,
GEO. CLINTON.

Gov. Clinton's force of about a thousand men, composed of the skeleton regiments of Colonels Samuel J.
Webb, DuBois, Sutherland and Ellison, with a part of
Hasbrouck's[1] and what remained of Lamb's artillery,
was instantly ordered to march through Shawangunk
and down the west side of the Waalkill. They crossed
the ferry where now stands the Rosendale bridge, making a hurried march and few halts ; in fact, it was too
rapid to leave the troops in any condition to fight,
should they reach the enemy's position. The route of
the column was on the Greenkill road, but only a portion of the advanced guard arrived at the *Kuykuyt*,
overlooking Kingston, to behold the village in flames
and the enemy nearly retired to his shipping. Had the
whole army been at hand it could not, of course, have
prevented the destruction of the village, or made any
serious resistance to the royal troops.

[1] Note VI.

The minutes of the Council sessions on the fifteenth consist of only a few lines—the time for personal effort on their part had come, and the Secretaries were engaged in something more stirring than clerkly labors, and only find leisure to note an order to impress 24 wagons to remove the military stores. Unfortunately all of these could not be procured and thus a considerable amount of public war-material was doomed to fall into the hands of the invaders.

It may be interesting to record the names of the members of the Council who were present on this day. They were Col. Van Courtlandt, Messrs. Dunscomb, Floyd, Van Zandt, Parks, Webster, Scott, Rowan, Harper, Pawling and Morris.

The utmost alarm existed and men were sending their families and such of their property as they could move, to Hurley and Marbletown. News came that the enemy's fleet had reached Esopus Island, only a few miles below the town landing, and it was evident that the worst hour was at hand. But in the midst of all this distress, for the too well known conduct of the royal generals forbade any hope of mercy from them, an express despatched in haste from Albany, brought the comforting assurance that the day was breaking in the north. It was conveyed in a letter from General Gates.[1]

Saratoga, Oct. 15th, 1777.

"Sir,

Inclosed I have the Honor to send your Excellency a Copy of my Letter of this Day to Major General Putnam, with a Copy of the Terms on which Lt. General Burgoyne has proposed to Surrender.

I am Sir,
Your Excellency's
Most Affectionate
Humble Servant,
HORATIO GATES."

His Excellency, Governor Clinton, Esq.

The terms of capitulation have been often printed and therefore need not be repeated.

This letter the Council lost no time in forwarding to New Windsor with this inclosure, also from the Clinton MSS.

---

[1] Clinton Papers in the N. Y. State Library.

Kingston, Oct. 15th, 1777, 5 p. m.

" Sir :

The enclosed is just come to hand by Express. We tho't it necessary to open it as it might contain matters which at this Critical Juncture we conceived we ought to know without Delay.

We just this moment have received information from the Landing that about thirty sail of the Enemy's Vessels appeared opposite the Esopus Island and Standing up the River. Some works have been thrown up below according to your Excellency's requisition. The alarm Gunns were just fired. We have not any particulars on this occasion more than already mentioned. We shall forward any further Information to you as it may from time to time occur without the loss of a moment. In the meantime give us leave, Sir, to assure you that we will contribute all in our power to enable the Militia Officers who command here to make the best possible Defence at this Post during your Excellency's absence.

I have the Honor to be

Your Excellency's

Most Ob't Serv't,

PIERRE VAN COURTLANDT,

Pres'dt.

His Excellency Governor Clinton."

Upon the receipt of General Gates' letter the Council voted the bearer of " good tidings " fifty dollars. The Governor did not receive it until some time after date, and the current story is, that it had been committed to a faithless messenger who stopped for the night at a farm house by the way side. He was found by another express leisurely setting out in the morning. He excused himself on the plea of his horse breaking down, which brought upon him all manner of reproaches from the good whig who had entertained him, and to whom no mention had been made of his order to make all possible effort to reach the reinforcements and urge them to press forward without a moment's delay.[1]

---

[1] I take this occasion to return my thanks for this and other interesting particulars connected with this sketch, obtained from Miss Margaret Wynkoop, a daughter of Judge Dirck Wynkoop, Jr., who figured much in these " troublous times." This venerable lady, whose

True to his word the stout-hearted Governor arrived at Kingston at about nine o'clock in the evening, and then sends off this dispatch [1] to Putnam on the other side of the river.

> "KINGS TOWN, 15th October, 1777,
> 10 o'clock Wednesday Evening.
>
> Dear General :
>
> What follows is the copy of a letter from the Chairman of the Committee of the city of Albany to the President of the Council of Safety. I congratulate you on the important intelligence contained in it.

To Gen. Putnam.

> ALBANY, 15th October, 1777.
>
> "Last night at 8 o'clock the capitulation whereby General Burgoyne and whole army surrendered themselves prisoners of War was signed, and this morning they are to march out towards the River above Fish Creek with the Honors of War, and there ground their Arms. They are from thence to be marched to Massachusetts Bay. We congratulate you on this happy event and remain."   Yours, &c.,
>   GEO. CLINTON."

With untiring energy and unabated zeal the Governor starts for Marbletown in the morning, where, finding that his fagged army cannot reach Kingston in time to be of any service, he directs the main body to proceed no farther. Issuing an order for the execution of Taylor, the spy, who had been carried along with the troops, he is back again at Kingston before noon, and at one o'clock writes to the Commandant at Albany : [2]

> "Sir :
>
> Read, seal and send forward the enclosed Letter. Use your discretion as to the contents. Take the most prudent measures with your Sick, Wounded and Pri-

---

elegant manners and refined tone lend such a charm to her society, still survives, at the age of 82, residing in the very house in Green street, where her father entertained General Washington on his visit to Kingston.

[1] Penn. Archives, V, p. 676.   [2] Clinton Papers.

souers. It is possible the Enemy may push on to Albany.

I am, Sir, your humble Servant."

GEO. CLINTON.

The following is the enclosure to Gen. Gates :

KINGSTON, 16th Oct., 1777, 1 o'clock.

Sir :

I am to inform you that the Enemy's **Fleet**, Consisting of upwards of thirty sail anchored last night about six miles below the Landing Place of this Town which they now lie directly opposite to, and appear to be making preparations for Landing. I have so few men with me that I can not say I have the best Prospect of making so good a Defence as might be wished. A Reinforcement is on the way to me which I left last night, and which I believe will not come up in season, and at any rate must be exceedingly fatigued. I am just informed that the Enemy are coming to the Land. I think it necessary to give you this information, that you may take such steps as may to you appear necessary to render their acquisition of this Town of as little importance as possible. I have the Honor to be

Your most obedient

&

humble servant.

GEO. CLINTON.

P. S. I most sincerely Congratulate you on your success Northward.

Let us now turn to the events of the memorable sixteenth of October.

The enemy who had remained at anchor near Esopus island the previous night, weighed on the morning of the 16th, and about nine o'clock drew up opposite the mouth of the Rondout creek, and the Point, and in a little while opened a vigorous cannonade upon the *Lady Washington* galley, lying in front of the present residence of Mr. George North, and the two batteries upon the high ground above Ponckhockie, afterwards called Breast-works hill. Five light pieces of cannon were in position in these hastily thrown up earthworks, and with a 32-pounder on the galley replied to the fire of the British ships, but without doing much damage. About one o'clock in the afternoon the troops in the

batteaux and boats of the naval vessels, were arranged
in two divisions and prepared to land; one division
consisting of about three or four hundred men proceeded
to Ponckhockie, near Radley's Ferry landing, and then
rapidly disembarked, and dispersed the men at the
batteries with the bayonet, the defenders of these works
remaining until the last moment, when they spiked their
guns and with a few wounded men withdrew in haste up
the creek. Only three houses stood where is now the
teeming throng of the busy village of Rondout — these
the invaders burnt, an occasional shot from the retreating militia, showing that it was only a lack of force
that prevented a vigorous resistance.

The boats immediately boarded and set fire to the
prison vessels and some sloops lying in the creek, which
task was somewhat impeded by the blowing up of a
quantity of powder in one of the store vessels. Lieut.
Clarke of the *Dependence*, and some of his crew were
injured by this explosion. The *Lady Washington* galley
was run up the creek and scuttled just below Eddy-
ville, and at South Rondout a party of the enemy's
seamen in pursuit of this vessel landed and destroyed
a house belonging to William Houghtaling, the only
damage done on the south side of the creek.

But it is time to look after the main body of the
enemy's troops, under Gen. Vaughan in person. This
division landed in a cove north of Columbus point and
near the brick-kiln, and took the direction of Kingston,
and on the top of the hill, not far from the late residence of H. H. Reynolds Esq., formed a junction with
the other party which had reached that spot by the
the " Strand road."

Here the column halted and Jacobus Lefferts,[1] a New
York tory temporarily residing in Kingston, approached
Gen. Vaughan and communicated to him the news of
the capitulation of Gen. Burgoyne at Saratoga. This
fact Gordon states on the authority of Mr. James Beek-
man,[2] and Major Van Gaasbeck, of Kingston, assures me
that he has heard that Lefferts was the informant, from
the lips of citizens who were in the village on that
fatal day. It has been said that no information of this
sort could have been received in Kingston at the time

---

[1] Jacobus Lefferts, Note VII.
[2] History, II, p. 579, note.

of the landing of the British, but this is an error. Gen. Burgoyne asked for a parley on the 13th of October, and one was actually held on the following day, in which the British commander offered to capitulate. Gen. Gates' letter to Gov. Clinton (see p. 26, *ante*), announcing this, was opened by the Council of Safety, sitting in the village, at 5 p. m., on the fifteenth. A letter from Jno. Barclay, chairman of the Albany county committee, with the same intelligence, was read at this meeting,[1] and although the announcement was somewhat premature, it was believed by all parties, and the clause omitted from Sir James Wallace's dispatch, published in the *London Gazette* of Dec. 2d, is corroborative of this view of the case.[2]

No information of the inutility of further attempts to create a diversion in favor of Burgoyne, could influence the leaders of this marauding expedition; they were bent on plunder and destruction, and the order to advance was speedily given. Lossing says that somewhere about this place they seized a negro and compelled him to pilot them to the town.

The only resistance they met with after leaving the vicinity of the water side was from a scattering fire kept up by a few men in and about the woods near the house of John O'Reilly. These men were quickly dispersed by the enemy's light companies, deployed as skirmishers, and by the parties on the flanks of the column, and although Vaughan's official report, and the servile Gazette of Rivington, speak of "firing from the houses," &c., it is the unanimous voice of tradition that no resistance whatever was made after the troops reached the vicinity of the village.

The militia, consisting of about 150 men, under the command of Colonels Levi Pawling and Johannes Snyder, could do nothing against such overwhelming odds, indeed, the largest portion was in the works at "the Strand," and so retreated up the Rondout creek—the inhabitants themselves were employed to the last in removing such of their effects as were portable, and abandoned their houses as the British troops entered the streets. It is to be remembered that many of those liable to do military duty were absent

---

[1] Jour. Prov. Conv., I, 1070, and the letter is at p. 28.
[2] See p. 34, *post*.

under arms with Gov. Clinton and in the northern army.

No time was to be lost by the invaders, for Governor Clinton's army could not be far off, and dividing into small parties they began to set fire to the houses in the village, showing particular spite in visiting the residences of leading whigs. So rapid had been the advance of the royal forces, that the records of the Dutch Church—and the missing cover of one of these venerable volumes is attributed to this haste—and some of the public papers in Mr. Bancker's charge at Judge Wynkoop's house, on the corner of Pearl and Fair streets (now of Mrs. S. Bruyn), were only removed a few moments before a party of red-coats began to plunder the buildings.

It did not take long to complete their work, and with the exception of the house and barn on the west side of Wall street, near the residence of Marius Schoonmaker, Esq., and then belonging to Tobias Van Steenburgh, every building in the village was destroyed. This long, one story stone dwelling is still standing, in good preservation, and belongs to Abram T. Van Steenburgh, a descendant of the revolutionary owner. Various reasons are given for their omission to set fire to these buildings. One New York newspaper says it was occupied by a Mrs. Hammersley—a tory lady in some way connected with the British officers. It is certain that a New York lady of this name was in Kingston about this time, and not unlikely occupied this house, but I have not been able to obtain any particulars in regard to her.

Some confusion in the newspaper accounts of that day has arisen, it being stated in Rivington's paper that the only house spared belonged to a Mr. Lefferts. Now, the house occupied by Mr. Lefferts was indeed saved from the flames, but it was some distance from the village proper, as stated in the appendix,[1] and could hardly be considered as belonging to it. The royal Gazette would no doubt soon learn that the house of so well known a sympathizer with the crown as Alderman Lefferts had not been burned.

I have heard that a party of soldiers proceeded towards this house in spite of the remonstrances of Mrs. Lefferts, whose bright red dress has been described by

[1] Note VII.

more than one informant, and were about to plunder it, when the sound of the recall hastened them back to the ranks. The north part of the house bears indisputable marks of being older than 1777.

The invaders destroyed a considerable quantity of arms and munitions of war, with flour and provisions stored here for the army, to say nothing of the property of the inhabitants, but I prefer to collect in one place the estimates of the enemy as to the amount of destruction they had been able to effect.

The stragglers of the royal army were gathered in as fast as possible, and with a quick step, in spite of all the booty they could carry away, not forgetting sundry negroes—for the British Anti-Slavery party had not yet been heard of—they set out for the river, and after an absence of about three hours reimbarked, having burned a defenceless village and made three or four thousand people houseless, and unable to recognize their homes in the ashes now heaped upon the spot where lately stood a flourishing town.

The following are the official accounts of the services performed by the British officers at Kingston :

ON BOARD THE FRIENDSHIP, OFF ESOPUS,
Friday, October 17, 10 o'Clock, Morning.[1]

Sir :

I have the Honor to inform you that on the Evening of the 15th Instant I arrived off Esopus; finding that the Rebels had thrown up Works and had made every Disposition to annoy us, and cut off our Communication, I judged it necessary to attack them, the Wind being at that Time so much against us that we could make no Way. I accordingly landed the Troops, attacked their Batteries, drove them from their Works, spiked and destroyed their Guns. Esopus being a Nursery for almost every Villain in the Country, I judged it necessary to proceed to that Town. On our Approach they were drawn up with Cannon which we took and drove them out of the Place. On our entering the Town they fired from their Houses, which induced me to reduce the Place to Ashes, which I accordingly did, not leaving a House. We found a considerable Quantity of Stores of all kinds, which shared the same Fate.

---

[1] London Gazette, Dec. 2d, 1777.

Sir James Wallace has destroyed all the Shipping except an armed Galley, which run up the Creek with every Thing belonging to the Vessels in Store.

Our Loss is so inconsiderable that it is not at present worth while to mention.

I am, &c.,

JOHN VAUGHAN.

GALLEYS AND ARMED VESSELS OFF ESOPUS CREEK, Oct. 17, 1777.[1]

Sir : We proceeded up the river, Destroying a number of vessels as we sailed along without stopping till we arrived at Esopus creek, where we found 2 batteries ; one of 2 guns, the other of 3 guns erected, and an armed Galley at the mouth of the Creek, who endeavored to prevent our passing by their Cannonade. Gen. Vaughan was of opinion that such a force should not be left behind. It was determined to land and destroy them, and immediately Executed, without retarding our proceeding up the River. The General marched for the town and fired it. The Boats from the armed vessels went up the Creek, Burnt 2 brigs, several armed sloops and other craft, with all their apparatus, that was in Stores upon the shore. Lieut. Clark of the " Dependence," with two or three others, in firing the stores was blown up, but we flatter ourselves not dangerously.

The officers and men upon this occasion behaved [with] the greatest spirit.

By all our information I am afraid that General Burgoyne is retreated if not worse.

I have, &c.

JAS. WALLACE.

Commodore Hotham.

Sir William Howe in his report to Lord George Germaine, dated Philadelphia, Oct. 25th, 1777, adds this Postcript :

" I have the satisfaction to enclose to your Lordship a report just rec'd of a very spirited piece of service performed by Major Genl. Vaughan, and Sir James Wallace, up the Hudson's River."

---

[1] Copy from the original in the Admiralty, London; this dispatch appeared in the *London Gazette* of Dec. 2d, 1777, with the omission of the last significant paragraph, which does not seem to have ever before been brought to public notice.

It has not been easy to procure the contemporary newspaper accounts of this expedition, at this late date, but such as have come to my notice are given, commencing with the royalist side.

Rivington's New York Gazette, October 27th, 1777.

Extract of a letter from Esopus, October 16th.

"On Monday evening we sailed from fort Montgomery, having first entirely demolished it, and blown up the magazine. We got up that night near Pollopel's Island, where we came to an anchor below the Cheveaux de Frize. Next morning, wind S. W., we weighed, got through the Cheveaux de Frize, and proceeded up the river. The towns of New Windsor and Newburgh appeared totally deserted by the inhabitants; four sloops set sail from Fishkill, but were soon overhauled by the gun boats, when opposite to Poughkeepsie; the rebels kept up a continual fire from the shore, without doing any damage, which was answered by the shipping. We anchored that night five miles from Esopus, and yesterday morning about nine o'clock a severe cannonade began between the shipping in front, and a row galley and two batteries the rebels had erected on shore. In the afternoon the troops landed at Esopus, attacked and took possession of the batteries, and, on marching up to the town, the rebels concealed in the houses, firing upon the troops from the windows, occasioned every house, except that of Alderman Lefferts of New York, to be set on fire and consumed: this was effected with the loss of only two men wounded. Many were burnt in the river and Esopus creek, besides some stores, a mill, &c."

New York Gazette, November 3d.

October 15 —"Three sloops taken, in attempting to escape to the Fishkill, and two pettiaugers, destroyed."

"The house, mill and outhouses, and a sloop belonging to Col. Francis Stoutenburgh, at Crum Elbow, burned. Two sloops on the east side, burnt that evening."

October 16.—Set fire to two brigs, &c., and burnt Kingston.

October 17.—"The house, store-house, barn, &c., of Mr. Petrus Ten Broeck, a rebel General, the house, barn, and out-houses of Robert Gilbert Livingston, and a house and mill belonging to Judge Livingston, on the east side of the river burned."

October, 18.—"Another house belonging to Judge Livingston, one to Mr. John Livingston, with three others, destroyed in like manner."

October 22.—"Two houses, one the property of Judge Smith, on the east side, a sloop and barn, likewise two houses, with their appendages on the west side, were burnt, and on the 23d a sloop was burned on the stocks.

In the town of Kingston, a large quantity of powder, and a large number of fire-arms, together with many valuable stores, were destroyed."   *   *   *

"Another more accurate Account from Esopus, informs us that on the landing of Gen. Vaughan with the Troops under his Command, the Rebels, without the least prospect of advantage to themselves, fired upon them from a Breastwork just thrown up, and which they did not stay to defend. This, joined to an insolent and provoking Behaviour occasioned the Army to march up and set fire to the Town, which was presently entirely consumed. There were destroyed Three Hundred and twenty-six houses, with a Barn to almost every one of them, filled with Flour, besides Grain of all kinds, much valuable Furniture and effects, which the Royal Army disdained to take with them. Twelve Thousand barrels of Flour were burnt, and they took at the town four pieces of Cannon, with ten more upon the River, with 1150 stand of Arms, with a large quantity of Powder were blown up. The whole Service was effected and the Troops re-embarked in three hours."

Independent Chronicle (Boston), October 30th.

Extract of a letter from Fishkill, dated October 19th :

"The enemy are upon the river, between this place and Albany. They have burnt Kingston (Esopus), not a house left standing in the town. It was a pretty compact place with several streets, 2 miles from the river, 60 miles from Albany, and the third town for size in this State. They also burnt several mills, stores, dwelling houses and vessels, as they advanced up the river However, they have something now in the way to stop their career: General Putnam is up with them on one side of the river, and our Governor on the other side; each of them have force sufficient to repel them, should they land."

Ibid., November 6th.

FISHKILL, October 24.

"Last Monday, our people took a small schooner belonging to the enemy, in the North River, near Rhynebeck, with a pretty valuable cargo; she ran aground, and our people took the advantage and boarded her with canoes. Nicholas James and George Hopkins, two of the New York pilots, were taken on board.

Last Thursday, one Taylor, a spy, was hanged at Hurley, who was detected with a letter to Burgoyne, which he swallowed in a silver ball, but by the assistance of a tartar emetic he discharged the same."

FISHKILL, October 30.

"Last Thursday, the fleet returned from their inglorious expedition up the North River, having burnt Kingston, in Esopus, and a few houses at Rhynebeck and Livingston's Manor, as was mentioned in our last; our army, commanded by Gen. Putnam, coming up with them, caused them to skulk on board their vessels, and prevented their doing further mischief; the wind being light in their return, which gave an opportunity to our army, of marching as fast as they sailed, and was an happy circumstance in our favor, and prevented them from destroying Poughkeepsie and other buildings on the river side."

New York Packet, October 23d.

October 14.—"Yesterday, General Vaughan, having under his command a large body of British, who have committed various acts of vandalism, in their passage up the North River, landed a number of men at Esopus, marched up to the defenceless town of Kingston, about two miles from the river, and immediately set it on fire. The conflagration was general in a few minutes, and in a very short time that pleasant and wealthy town was reduced to ashes; one house only escaped the flames. Thus by the wantonness of power the third town in New York for size, elegance and wealth, is reduced to a heap of rubbish, and the once happy inhabitants (who are chiefly of Dutch descent) obliged to solicit for shelter among strangers; and those who lately possessed elegant and convenient dwellings, obliged to take up with such huts as they can find to defend them from the cold blasts of approaching winter We learn that the inhabitants saved the best part of their movable property; but some lost the great part of their temporal all. 'Tis said the enemy took little plunder, being told that Governor Clinton was at hand with fifteen hundred men, but unluckily not so near as to save the town. They burnt several houses at Rhynebeck Flats, and proceeded as far as Livingston Manor, where they burnt a few more. Our troops are now up with them. It is hoped that they will be able to put a stop to these depredations. Britain, how art thou fallen! Ages to come will not be able to wipe away the guilt, the horrid guilt, of these and such like deeds, lately perpetrated by thee."

The Americans did not think it expedient to make any official statement of the amount of their losses in stores and munitions of war, and while the account of the enemy's success in their destruction is probably exaggerated, there is no room to doubt that the State suffered heavily on this occasion.

The county records escaped the fire, but some portions now missing may not have been brought back to Kingston after the Rochester journey. The "minutes" of the Kingston Trustees for the year 1777 were destroyed with the papers of Christopher Tappen, their clerk, as appears from an entry in their books in his own handwriting.

The injury done to the inhabitants was more than most of them could well bear; many persons in comfortable and even affluent circumstances were reduced to almost absolute want, and all were forced to seek shelter at some distance from their late pleasant homes.

The conduct of the cruel foe met with an indignant cry from all parts of the continent, and it steeled the hearts and nerved the arms of our countrymen to pursue with unabating energy the course of resistance to British Tyranny.

When the news of the destruction of Kingston reached Gen. Gates, now the victor of Saratoga, he addressed the following spirited letter[1] to Gen. Vaughan, which was forwarded in the boat carrying Lord Petersham with Burgoyne's Dispatches to Sir Henry Clinton.

"ALBANY, 19th October, 1777.

Sir,

With unexampled cruelty you have reduced the fine village of Kingston to Ashes, and most of the wretched Inhabitants to ruin. I am also informed you continue to ravage, and burn all before you on both sides of the River. Is it thus your King's General thinks to make Converts to the Royal Cause?

It is no less surprising than true, that the measures they adopt to serve their master have quite the contrary effect.

Their Cruelty establishes the glorious act of Independency upon the broad basis of the general resentment of the people.

Other Generals and much older officers than you can pretend to be are now by the fortune of War in my hands; their fortune may one day be yours, when, Sir, it may not be in the power of anything human to save you from the just vengeance of an injured people.

I am, Sir,

Y^r most obed^t hum. Servt

HORATIO GATES."

The Honorable John Vaughan, Maj^r General.

Sympathy for the misfortunes of the people of Kingston came in resolves and donations from various parts of the country, but one of the most substantial testimonies of good feeling appears in a letter to Governor Clinton written on behalf of citizens of South Carolina.

"CHARLES TOWN, 31st March, 1778.

Sir :

I do myself the Pleasure to send you herewith the sum of £3711.10. equal to £927.17.6 New York currency. This money has been received for the charitable purpose of alleviating the distresses of the now indigent inhabitants of the Town of Kingston, who by the ravages of the Enemy are reduced to poverty and want. A much larger sum would have been collected had not

<hr>

[1] In Gen. Gates' Letter to Congress, Oct 20, 1777, published by order of Congress.

a melancholy accident by fire called the immediate
attention of many liberal souls to dissipate the wants of
many of the Inhabitants of the capital of this State,
who are reduced to beggary by the late Dreadful Conflagration.

From a Personal acquaintance with your Excellency, I persuade myself you will readily excuse the
trouble I give in requesting your attention to a proper
distribution of this donation. I have the pleasure to be
with sentiments of esteem and respect,

Your most Obedient Hum'l Serv't,
ADM. LIVINGSTON."
His Excellency George Clinton.

Among the papers of the Trustees of Kingston,
now in the Ulster County Clerk's office, is the following
letter from Robt. R. Livingston. It is dated March 1st,
1778.

" Gent.—
The inconvenience I daily Experience from the
destruction of my house and the ravages of the Enemy
serve only to increase my sympathy with the Inhabitants of Kingston and animate my desire in proportion
as they lessen my power to contribute to their relief as
liberally as I wish. My inattention to my private
affairs for three years past and the disaffection of my
Tenants who have during this controversary very generally withheld their Rents, put it out of my power to
contribute what might perhaps be of more immediate
use to my distressed friends at Kingston. Yet I flatter
myself that my present proposal may meet with their
approbation and be attended with permanent advantage and in this view I am induced to make it. I mean
a grant of 3000 acres of Land in any part of Hardenburgh's Pattent that falls to my share—which I promise
to make to the Trustees for the use of the inhabitants
thereof under the following restrictions. 1st, to be
taken in a regular square. 2d, not to be located at
Woodstock or Shandakan, nor at any other place on
which a settlement has been made—and that the Loca-
tion be made within three months from the date hereof
and a survey thereof returned in order to perfect the
grant. This Land the Trustees will dispose of in such

way as will be most advantageous to the suffering Inhabitants of Kingston.

As I have been informed that many of them have been disappointed in not being able to procure Boards, I have prevailed upon my Mother to suffer Mr. Saxe to dispose of all but her third which she reserves for her own use. I shall be happy if this or anything else in my power can in the least contribute to the ease or convenience of those whose attention to me early in life entitles them to my Friendship and who are more endear'd by the generous cause in which they suffer.

I am Gentl^m

With great regard

Your most Obed^t Hum. Servt

RODT. R LIVINGSTON."

This offer was accepted by the Trustees and the land located mostly in Great Lot No. 40 of the *Hardenbergh Patent*, now in Middletown, Delaware County. A survey of it was made by Wm. Cockburn in 1784, and the settlement on this tract is still known as New Kingston. It was equally divided by the Trustees among 100 families of the sufferers by the burning of the village.

Gov. Clinton concentrated his little force at Hurley, and did not follow the enemy lest he might be shut in between the Catskill Mountains and the river should the British land in force. His first letter to General Gates and another to General Putnam have been preserved.

"MARBLE TOWN, 17th Octr 1777.[1]

Dr. General :

Yesterday afternoon about four o'clock, the Enemy took Possession of and burnt the Town of Kingston. For want of a proper number of troops no effectual Resistance could be made. I have now the Body of men under my Command which marched from New Windsor to my assistance and shall immediately proceed to the Ruins of Kingston which the Enemy have abandoned. I have sent off a Party of Light Horse to reconnoitre and shall act in such manner as the motions of the Enemy may direct. I heard that General Burgoyne had surrendered and am very sorry

---

[1] Gates Papers.

to find by your Letter that Nothing has been done but to interchange of Proposals but I hope that matter is by this time concluded.

I have the Honor to be

Sir

Your most ob'dt

&

Humble Servt.

GEO. CLINTON.

P. S. A prisoner who is by no means intelligent says that the enemy are two thousand strong commanded by Gen. Vaughan."

Gov. Clinton to Gen. Putnam.

"HURLEY, Oct. 18th, 1777.[1]

Dear Sir,

I am this moment favored with yours of this morning. There is nothing new happened in this Quarter since I wrote you yesterday. The Enemy is 8 or 10 Miles above this burning away, but as there are no Capital Settlements there on this side the River and the situation of the Country such as with my present Force I can't advance opposite to them with safety to my Artillery. I mean at present to continue where I now am in Front of the most Valuable settlements and where the Stores and Effects from Kingston are removed. I imagine the Enemy will not proceed much higher up the River and that on their return they will attempt to lay waste the places they have passed going up, after our Troops are drawn from them. This induces me to think some more Troops ought to be left, at Poughkeepsie and Fishkill, but of this you can best judge. Adieu. You shall hear of me frequently.

Your most obed't Serv't.

GEO. CLINTON."

Gen. Putnam's letter to Gov. Clinton announces that he is again *preparing* to be of some service, which preparations do not seem to have resulted in any damage to the enemy, so far as it related to his operations on the east bank. Gov. Clinton was a more dangerous foe.

"LEROYR, STATEFORD, 18th Oct. 1777.[1]
5 O'clock Saturday Morning.

Dear Sir,

Yours of the 17th I received last night, and am sorry to hear of the Enemys Destroying the several Houses, &c. Last night I arrived here and all the Troops, Excepting General Sullivans Brigade, which I Expect will join me this morning. Colonel Samuel Willis with his Regiment are about six miles a Head. I am just seting off and this morning Expect to reach the Shipping. Last Night I received a Letter from Colonel Willis by whom I am informed that from every appearance the Enemy mean to Burn the Powder Mills, &c. He further adds from the best Intelligence he's able to Procure from the Inhabitants they mean if possible to penetrate to Sailsbury. If that scheam should take place, I flatter myself we shall be able to give a good acc'. of 'em. I apprehend we shall find it very difficult to convey the necessary Intelligence to each other, but at every opportunity shall be glad to know your situation In order that we may act in junction. Am in haste.

D' Sir
Your very humb'' Serv',
ISRAEL PUTNAM."

We can not have a better view of the situation of matters in the vicinity of Kingston, than will be found in Governor Clinton's letter to Gen. Gates.

"HURLY 2 Miles, and a half from Kingston, Oct. 21, 1777.[2]

Dear Sir,

I have repeatedly done myself the honor, to inform you of my situation, and think it my Duty again to do so, that if any of those consequences should happen, which may now be easily foreseen, the blame, if any, may not lie at my Door.

When I undertook at the request of Genl. Putnam, to put myself at the head of a body of men to protect the Western Shores of Hudson's River, and

---

to throw myself between the Enemy and your army, should they proceed up the River, I represented to him in strong terms the situation of this part of the Country thinly inhabited, and the interior part unsettled, and separated from all assistance by a chain of mountains. In consequence of which representation, he agreed to let me have three thousand men, if the Eastern Militia should come in, as he expected they would, of which number however he hath not sent four hundred. I then clearly saw that it would be impossible for me, to protect the country, unless I could be reinforced from the Northern Army, which from your letter I had reason to expect : I wrote also to Genl. Dickenson of New Jersey upon the same subject, and I am inform'd, that he, notwithstanding the exposed situation of his own State, has ordered six hundred men to my brother's assistance at New Windsor. Kingston hath been destroy'd, merely because I have been so deceiv'd in my expectations of assistance, that it was impossible to take measures for its Security.

I am now Sir, at the head of little more than one thousand men, to cover the most valuable part of the County of Ulster.

The Enemy have lain still yesterday, and the day before, with a strong southerly wind, from whence it is evident, that a knowledge of Burgoyne's Fate hath chang'd their intentions against Albany. If they land in Force I must either retreat, or sacrifice my few men and lose seven very valuable pieces of field artillery. If I retreat this whole County will be ravag'd and destroy'd, and that [at] a Season of the year. when the Inhabitants (who are warmly attached to the American Cause) will want time to provide cover for their Families against the inclemencies of the ensuing Winter.

While we act merely on the defensive, two thousand men on the River will find full employment for twelve or fifteen. But if four thousand are left to cover Albany, two thousand here, and two thousand on the other side of the river, it will be by no means impracticable, to recover the Passes in the Highlands, in which case the greater part of the army, now along the Banks of the River may be brought to act offensively against the Enemy, and perhaps render the present Campaign decisive in our favor.

Col. Malcolm who is the Bearer of this letter, will

do himself the honor of stating and explaining to you my Ideas upon this subject; and you will do me a particular favor, if in answer to this, you will inform me what I am to expect, and what is expected from me.

I am Dr Genl with particular Esteem,

Your most obt Servant,

GEO. CLINTON."

To the Honble. Major Genl. Gates Albany.

The British Squadron remained at anchor the night of the sixteenth, and on Friday morning a strong party landed and burnt some houses at the village of Rhinebeck, and plundered the inhabitants in the vicinity. A vessel dispatched down the river to convey the reports of Gen. Vaughan and Sir James Wallace, grounded near Poughkeepsie and fell into the hands of the Americans, as narrated in a letter from Gen. Putnam to Gen. Gates.

"HEAD QUARTERS Red Hook 20th October, 1777.[1]

Dr General,

Your favor of the 19th I have just receiv'd and I beg leave to congratulate you upon the great success you have met with in your Department. Yesterday a Pilot Boat was detached from the Enemy's Fleet (wch Lays Opposite this) with Despatches to N. York, but the Boat happening to get on ground near to Poughkeepsie, gave our Troops (which are there stationed) an opportunity of Boarding her. The Inclos'd you have Copy's of the Letters which was On Board. You'll observe from Vaughans Letter to General Clinton that they with their small Craft Intend Proceeding up the River.

On the 18th inst I arrived here, and yesterday I arranged and posted my Troops in such a manner as I think will effectually prevent them from Landing: before I arriv'd, they burnt Esopus & a number of Buildings along the Shore.

If your situation would admit I should be exceeding glad you would Immediately send me some heavy Cannon (upon Traveling Carriages) with ammunition &c compleat—in their present situation they might be annoy'd greatly, and not only so but We could distress

[1] Gates Papers

them very much should they attempt Passing up the
River—if you have no particular object in view, should
be glad you would send down all the Continental Troops
you can conveniently spare, as the Militia I have now
with me are very troublesome and anxious to get Home.
I need not mention to you the Reasons they assign, as
you well know the disposition of that People.

From the Inclosed Letters it appears they meant to
reinforce Burgoyne, but thank God you have prevented
that.   When they learn the news about Burgoyne, their
scheam of making a junction is no more, but you may
depend that they will Indeavour to Proceed up the
River and destroy all the Buildings, &c. they Possible
can, but I hope your timely assistance will prevent 'em ;
from the best Intelligence I have been able to get of
late they Enemy's as not more than three thousand on
Board.

Am in haste,
Dr General
Your very humble Servt.
ISRAEL PUTNAM."

To Major Gen. Gates, Albany.

Copies of the intercepted dispatches are among the
Gates Papers, and the autograph of Sir James Wallace,
in Lossing's *Field Book.* bears a striking resemblance to
the signature at the bottom of this letter.   Can it be a
mistake ?

" LIVINGSTON'S MILLS, N. River,
October 18th, 1778.

Sir,
Inclos'd is the best intelligence we can get of Mr.
Burgoyne.

We are not certain what is become of the arm'd
Rebel Galley, as Esopus Creek is 3 Mile Navigable, and
Night coming on before we could explore the whole of
it.   therefore would it not be proper for some Frigate
or arm'd vessel to be thereabouts, to secure ye Navigation of ye River—We cannot properly spare any from
the army—Ammunition is wanted among ye arm'd vessels.

I have ye Honor to be, Sir,
Your most Humble Servant
JAS. WALLACE.

P. S. Every opportunity will be taken to send to
Mr. Burgoyne.
    Commodore Hotham.
                    (A true copy).

The Intelligence alluded to in the foregoing part of
this letter, being inserted in that from General Vaughan
to General Clinton, it was tho't unnecessary to trans-
cribe it again."
Endorsed in Gen. Gates' handwriting :
    " Intercepted letter from Capt. Wallace to Commo^c
Hotham, dated 18th October, 1777."

" *Information of Gilead Bettus 18th Oct 1777,*

who says that he was taken Prisoner by the Rebels on
Monday the 6th inst. That the following day there was
a battle between the King's Troops and the Rebels, with
the loss our side of 7 or 8 Pieces of Cannon, about 150,
amongst whom General Fraser killed, and 150 mostly
Hessians taken Prisoners, that General Burgoyne retreated the same Night leaving behind 300 Sick and
300 Barrels of Provisions and that a brigade of rebels
marched the next day, the 8th to intercept the retreat
of General Burgoyne.

That on Saturday last there was another Engage-
ment, in which the King's Troops killed near 100 of the
Rebels, without any loss, that Genl Burgoyne was, to
the best of his knowledge, at Saratoga last Monday
which was thirty-six miles from Albany, and says that
heard Cannon last Tuesday but knew no Particulars,
and further says that when he was taken Prisoner, but
five Hessians had deserted from the King's Troops, but
that the Rebels deserted to them in great numbers.

Dear Sir,

I shall send off this night to Gen' Burgoyne at the
same time I desire to inform you that all the armed
Ships are in want of ammunition, that it will be abso-
lutely necessary for a Frigate to lay off Esopus for the
reasons mentioned by Sir J. Wallace to the Commodore,
that the Heavy Ships cannot get nearer than 46 Miles
to Albany but that the smaller ones will proceed higher
up.

It is reported that the Rebels Army near Albany amounts to 18000 men.

I am

Dear Sir

Your most obedᵗ &

Humble Servant

JOHN VAUGHAN.

From on Board the Friendship off Livingston's Mills *that were*,¹ Saturday 18 Octʳ 1777, Morning 10 o'clock."

(True copy.)   C. TILLINGHAST."

Endorsed in Gen. Gates' handwriting:

" Intercepted letter from M. G. Vaughan to Lt. G. Sir Henry Clinton, dated Livingston's Mills, 18 Octʳ 1777."

Of course Gen. Vaughan could not hope, after the intelligence of Burgoyne's disaster at Saratoga, to make much further effort to the northward, and moving up the river, lay off Saugerties until the 23d, landing detachments from time to time and destroying the powder mills at Livingston's manor and the houses of Chancellor Livingston, Mrs. Montgomery, and doing other damage, as related by a writer in a newspaper before cited.

On their return they came to, opposite Kingston on the evening of the 23d ; on the following morning sailed down the river, and in the afternoon of that day they passed the Chevaux-de-frize at New Windsor and rejoined the forces in the Highlands.

The result of the expedition did not satisfy the loyalists in America or England ; they complained bitterly of the dilatory policy of Sir Henry Clinton and General Vaughan, and seemed to think that they could easily have accomplished the sixty miles' sail and made themselves masters of Albany It is quite likely this could have been done for there were no troops of any account in that city, but General Vaughan heard of the fate of the Northern army, and felt assured that his return to New York might, in the event of his going higher, prove a difficult matter, and therefore did not

¹ Underscored in the paper quoted, and showing the *animus* of these valiant marauders.

chose to hazard his own reputation as a military commander by a desperate effort to save his fellow soldier at Saratoga. Gen. Vaughan has also asserted that a contrary wind prevented his further advance—an assertion not borne out by the opposite statement of Gov. Clinton, that a " strong southerly wind " was blowing. I have a copy of the log-book of the " Preston," which, it will be remembered, remained near the forts of the Highlands, and southerly winds are noted in the register as having prevailed on the days mentioned in the Governor's letter. There certainly was a head wind on the 17th and 18th of October, when the squadron were getting up to Saugerties, but not afterwards, so it was the news from Burgoyne, which prevented General Vaughan from advancing, not the wind.

On the morning of the 18th the troops witnessed the execution of Taylor, the spy, at Hurley. As soon as possible Gen. Gates dispatched two brigades southward, and after the enemy had dropped down the river the whole force moved to New Windsor and to join Gen. Washington in the Jerseys.

The first session of the Court of Common Pleas of Ulster County, after the fire, commenced at the house of Johannes Tack, Inn-holder, in Marbletown, May 5th, 1778

Levi Pawling, Dirck Wynkoop, Jr., Judges; Johannes Sleght, Nathan Smith and Patrick Barber, Assistant Justices.

The Council of Safety, dispersed at the burning of Kingston, did not meet again until the 19th of October at the house of Andrew Oliver in Marbletown, when the following preamble and resolution was passed :

" Whereas, The late destruction of the town of Kingston, and a vast number of dwelling houses, improvements, grain and fodder on each side of Hudson's river, by a cruel—inhuman and merciless enemy, has deprived many persons and families, the good subjects of this State, of shelter and subsistance for themselves and their cattle—calamities which, by the blessing of God on the fruits of this land, those who have not shared in so uncommon a misfortune, are enabled, in a great measure, to relieve

Resolved, therefore, That it be, and it is hereby, most earnestly recommended to the several and respective general and district committees of the counties of

Ulster, Dutchess, Orange and Westchester, to make or cause to be made a proper and proportionate distribution of the aforesaid distressed persons and families, and their cattle, to the end that they may all be provided for, as the circumstances of the country will permit; and it is hereby most strenuously urged on all those who may not have shared with them in their afflictions, to receive the aforesaid persons, families and cattle, and furnish them with shelter and subsistence at a moderate rate."

The sessions of the Council continued at Marbletown until November 18th, when they adjourned to Hurley, meeting at the house of Capt. Jan Van Densen until the 17th of December. After this date it ceased to meet in Ulster County, but resumed business at Poughkeepsie, December 22d, 1777.

The Supreme Court, which opened for the first time on the 9th of September, with an able charge from Chief Justice Jay, which was printed in Holt's paper, and is found in his life by Wm. Jay, had adjourned before the attack.

And here terminates the sketch of the Expedition of Gen. Vaughan, but I may be permitted to recall the pleasant change in public sentiment, which the lapse of three-quarters of a century has brought about. This very morning, not two hours since, the grandson of that king, George the Third, whom our fathers so much detested, was honored with a salute from the cannon of the organized militia of this county, successors of the men of 1777, and fired, too, from the very spot where eighty-three years ago, at the same hour, the guns of Pawling's redoubts were speeding messengers of death into the royal squadron. May this visit of the Prince of Wales serve to increase that harmony, which should ever exist among the great members of the Anglo-Saxon race, " Creation's priests and kings !"

APPENDIX.

7

APPENDIX

NOTES AND DOCUMENTS.

— ◦◦◦◦◦ — —

NOTE I.

SIR JAMES WALLACE.

Is found as a Lieutenant, March 11th, 1755, and became a Commander in 1762 — was made a Post Captain, June 10th, 1771. In command of the Rose, 20 gun frigate, he was stationed at Newport during the winters of 1774-75, and particularly annoyed the inhabitants of Rhode Island by the detention of their shipping and constant attempts to carry off their live stock, &c. On this account a spirited correspondence took place between Governor Cooke and Captain Wallace, but Arnold in his *History of Rhode Island* (II. p. 351,) has preserved a more laconic one, which he had with Commodore Whipple of the new Continental navy. Whipple had been a leader in the famous attack upon the British schooner Gaspee, burned not far from Providence ; on learning this, Wallace addressed the following epistle to him :

" You, Abraham Whipple, on the 10th of June, 1772, burned His Majesty's vessel, the Gaspee, and I will hang you at the yard arm
JAMES WALLACE."

The answer was equally short and pithy :

" To Sir James Wallace, Sir—Always catch a man before you hang him.
ABRAHAM WHIPPLE."

Not long after this Sir James bombarded the town of Bristol, in Rhode Island. In 1777 he had command of the *Experiment*, 50 gun frigate, and afterwards served in the *Nonsuch*, 64. He saw much service upon the American coast during the revolution, and was thoroughly detested for the severity with which he carried out the orders of the King's government. A characteristic anecdote of his brutality and the severe retort of a Philadelphia Quaker, is in Graydon's *Memoirs*, p. 76. April 12th, 1794, he became a rear-admiral ; a vice-admiral June 1st, 1795, and on the 1st of January, 1801, was made an admiral of the Blue. He distinguished himself in several actions, and in the latter part of his life was appointed Governor of Newfoundland. Died in London, March 6th, 1803. (*Gent Mag.* — *Navy List, &c.*)

Note II.

GEN. VAUGHAN.

The Hon. John Vaughan, the second son of Wilmot, 3d Visconnt
Lisburne, entered the army in 1746, as a cornet in the 10th dragoons,
and in 1756 appears as a captain in the 17th regiment of foot. While a
lieutenant colonel he commanded a division of grenadiers at the capture of Martinique, and distinguished himself on that occasion. On the
11th of May, 1775, he succeeded to the colonelcy of the 46th regiment,
then ordered on service in America, and there he acted as Brigadier and
Major General, having the local rank of the last grade from Jan. 1st,
1776, and the full commission on the British establishment from Aug.
29th, 1777. Gen. Vaughan was wounded in the thigh shortly after the
landing on Long Island, and for a time disabled from active service.
Commanding in the right column of attack upon Forts Clinton and
Montgomery, his horse was killed under him, and he is thus particularly noticed in Sir Henry Clinton's orders, of Oct. 7th, 1777: "Fort
Montgomery is henceforth to be distinguished by the name of Fort
Vaughan, in memory of the intrepidity and noble perseverance which
Major General Vaughan showed in the assault of it." The second expedition up the Hudson and the barbarous destruction of Kingston, will
keep the name of Vaughan in lively remembrance in the State of New
York. After his services on the continent we next hear of him in the
office of commander-in-chief of the forces in the Leeward Islands, where,
in conjunction with Admiral Rodney, he took St. Eustatius, and some
proceedings there brought out a smart debate in the House of Com-
mons.

Gen. Vaughan was appointed governor of Fort William, in Scotland,
but shortly afterwards obtained the more lucrative post of Berwick and
Holy Island. He represented Berwick in four successive parliaments,
and became a Lieutenant General in 1782 In 1793, the government
conferred upon him the Order of the Bath, and on the 30th of June,
1795, Gen. Vaughan died suddenly, and not without suspicion of
poison, in the island of Martinique. He was unmarried, and at the
time of his death had attained his 57th year. (Gent. Mag. — Army
List., &c.)

Note III.

DANIEL TAYLOR, THE SPY.

Daniel Taylor, a first lieutenant, in Captain Stewart's company of the
9th regiment of the Royal Army, as he says in his confession, was
arrested on the 10th of October, in the neighborhood of Little Britain,
Orange county, by a picket guard of Col. Webb's regiment, under the
command of Lieut. Howe It seems that he was deceived by the uniform of the party, who were clothed in red coats, which had been
recently captured in a British transport. Some of them had been dyed
blue—the regimental uniform—but time did not permit the whole parcel
to be so changed, and they were served out in their original sanguinary
hue. Asking the name of the commanding general, he was answered,
General Clinton, into whose presence, at his own request he was con-
ducted. There, instead of Sir Henry, the royal commander, he found
the republican governor, George Clinton, and he was immediately
observed to put something into his mouth. But the story will be best

old in the following extract from a letter of Gov. Clinton to the Council of Safety, dated "Mrs. Falls, 11th October, 1777" (Jour. Prov. Conv., I. p 1068) :

"The letter from Clinton to Burgoyne, taken from Daniel Taylor, was inclosed in a small silver ball of an oval form, about the size of a fusee bullet, and shut with a screw in the middle. When he was taken and brought before me he swallowed it I mistrusted this to be the case, from information I received, and administered to him a very strong emetic calculated to act either way. This had the desired effect ; it brought it from him ; but though close watched, he had the art to conceal it a second time.

I made him believe I had taken one Capt. Campbell, another messenger who was out on the same business ; that I learned from him all I wanted to know, and demanded the ball on pain of being hung up instantly and cut open to search for it, This brought it forth "

The contents of this letter was as follows:

"FORT MONTGOMERY, October 8th, 1777.

"Nous y voici, and nothing now between us but Gates I sincerely hope this little success of ours may facilitate your operations In answer to your letter of the 28th Sept., by C. C., I shall only say, I cannot presume to order, or even advise, for reasons obvious. I heartily wish you success. Faithfully yours,

Gen. Burgoyne. H. CLINTON "

The C. C. mentioned in the letter was another spy (Captain Campbell), who left the Highlands with a similar message, and more fortunate than Taylor, actually reached General Burgoyne on the 16th of the month.

This bullet belonged formerly to Gen. James Talmadge, and was exhibited at a meeting of the New York Historical Society, in 1843. It is said to be now in the possession of Charles A. Clinton, Esq., and that the writing upon the slip of paper which was inclosed therein is nearly obliterated

In Eager's *History of Orange County*, we are told that Dr. Moses Highy, who then resided at "the Square," administered the emetic which afforded such convincing proof of Taylor's employment.

Taylor was, of course, detained in custody, and on the 14th a General Court Martial met for his trial

"At a general Court Martial held at the heights of New Windsor the 14th October, 1777, by order of Brigadier General George Clinton, whereof Colonel Lewis Duboyse was President

Major Bradford,	Capt. Galespie.
Major Huntington,	Capt. Conklin,
Capt. Savage,	Capt. Wood,
Capt. Watson,	Capt. Hamtramk,
Capt. Wyllis,	Capt. Lee,
Capt. Ellis,	Capt. Huested.

Daniel Taylor, charged with lurking about the camp as a spy from the enemy, confined by order of General Clinton, was brought before said court, and to the above crime the prisoner plead not guilty. But confessed his being an Express from General Clinton to General Burgoyne, when taken. And that he had been employed as an Express also, from General Burgoyne to General Clinton, and was taken in the Camp of the Army of the United States near New Windsor, by Lieut. Rowe. Taylor likewise confessed his being a first Lieutenant in Captain Stewart's Company in the 9th Regiment of the British Troops, and but one man in company when taken The prisoner plead that he was not employed as a spy, but on the contrary was charged both by General Clinton and Burgoyne not to come near our Camp ; but meeting accidentally with some of our troops, in British Uniform, he was thereby deceived and discovered himself to them.

The Court after considering the case, were of opinion that the prisoner is guilty of the charge brought against him, and adjudged him to suffer death, to be hanged at such time and place as the General shall direct.

A true copy of the proceedings: Test.

LEWIS DUBOYS, *Col.*,
President."*

In the Clinton Papers is another Document, viz:

" *The confession of Daniel Taylor at New Windsor. Oct.* 9, 1777.

I left Fort Montgomery yesterday evening with a charge from General Clinton to go to General Burgoyne and acquaint him that he had landed about five miles below the Fort, clambered over the mountains, and stormed with small arms the back part of the Fort, which he carried with the loss of Lt Colo Grant, of Regt Volunteers, Major Campbell, Major Sela, (*Sill*) a number other officers and about 300 rank and file, that the obstructions in the river were now nearly removed and that he, Genl Burgoyne, might now move forward or go back, and to acquaint him that Genl Howe was near Philadelphia, and had defeated the Rebels; and that the Frigates belonging to the Rebels in the River were both burnt.

A Capt Campbell had come from Genl Burgoyne to Genl Clinton with dispatches, and set of on his return, on Tuesday morning ye 7th inst.

I left Genl Burgoyne 6 mile above Fort Edward the last of July, with orders to acquaint the commanding Officer in New York, that the Roads were so broke up it was extremely difficult, but so soon as he could clear the way he should advance.

I was likewise to inform Genl Burgoyne that they had now the Key of America (say the passes thro' the Highlands of Hudson's River.)"

When the little army of Governor Clinton moved down the Walkill to save Kingston, Taylor was taken along, his name appearing every day in the guard reports In the interval of a short halt it seems the Governor found time to consider the case, if indeed, it required much consideration, after the interview at Little Britain, and the following General Order issued on the morning of the destruction of Kingston determined his fate.

" Head Quarters, at Marble Town,
16th October, 1777.

The sentence of the General Court Martial whereof Cole DuBois was President, against the within named Daniel Taylor is approved and ordered to be carried into execution, when the troops are paraded and before they march to morrow morning.

GEO. CLINTON, B. Genl,
Continental Army "

It was not, however, carried into effect on the 17th, as directed ; no doubt the attention of the troops was taken up with matters at Kingston. He was still under guard on the morning of the 18th, when his name ceases to trouble the officer in charge.

In a MS. journal kept by a person in Clinton's force, which has been communicated to me by Mr. Jonathan W. Hasbrouck, is this entry :

---

* Clinton Papers.

"18, Saturday. Mr. Taylor, a spy taken in Little Brittain, was hung here. Mr. Romain and myself attended him yesterday, and I have spent ye morning in discoursing to him, and attended him at ye gallows. He did not appear to be either a political or a gospel penitent."

Tradition has it that Taylor was hanged on an apple tree near the village of Hurley.

Among the articles found on his person, and now preserved in the Clinton papers, in the State Library, are two letters from soldiers in the British army at New York, from which it may be supposed that Taylor came from the neighborhood of Kinderhook in Columbia county.

"Mr Daniel Taylor Sir i am glad to hear that you are come in safe again i hear you are a going home ward i have Roght a few Lines to my wife and my brother witch they will understand and i hope it will not indanger you. rap up some small things in it as tho it was sume old paper. Your brother John is not well this from your frend."

JOSIAH WOODWARD."

"KINGS BRIDGE July 31st 1777

Mr Daniel Taylor Sir these are to let you know I am well as all that came from Kinderhook Except your Brothers John. Joseph. peter are something Poorly. but are all able to walk. I have nothing strance to Wright Sir I Desere you would take the trouble to Wright to me and Let me Know the state of a falrse in our Naber Whood of our famalyes and frinds that came from Kenderhook. for I hear that you are a going Northard once more and if you arive to Kinderhook We all Desere you to Let our famiies Know how we all are Sir Be so kind as to Wright to some frind in our Nabourhood that they may have sertain Inteligence I would have wrote to my wife but I thought you would not chuse to carry a letter Remember us to all Enquiring frinds. So I remain your frind till Death. BENJ. INGRAHAM in
To Mr Daniel Taylor Capt Taget Company."

Whether this is the same Taylor who had been before arrested as a Tory, as appears from the List of N. Y. State prisoners, confined at Philadelphia, from Oct., 1776, to January, 1777 (Jour. Prov. Conv. I, p. 1000), may be a matter of conjecture.

NOTE IV.

MEMBERS OF CONGRESS AND THE LEGISLATURE.

JAMES CLINTON.—A biographical sketch may be found in Ruttenber's *Obstructions to the Navigation of Hudson's River*, p. 99, and a portrait in Irving's Washington, 5th Edition.

GOVERNOR GEORGE CLINTON.—See Street's *Council of Revision*, for the fullest account of this revolutionary worthy.

COL. JOHANNES HARDENBERGH —Son of the patentee of the "Hardenbergh Patent," was a member of the Colonial Assembly from 1737 to 1743, and again of the State Legislature in 1781 and '82. He held the post of Colonel in the first regiment of the county militia for upwards of 20 years and died Aug. 29th, 1786, aged 80 years and 2 months. The Hasbrouck MS. diary, notes that "he was a true and sincere friend to Church and State. He was about 6 feet 2 or 3 inches high, walked straight and upright, well proportioned of body, light eyes of a grayish cast, light brown hair."

When Gen. Washington visited the county in June, 1783, Col. Hardenbergh entertained Mrs. Washington, with Governor and Mrs. Clinton, at breakfast, at his house in Rosendale —a substantial edifice, of but little architectural pretensions, which was recently the residence of Mr. Cornell.

Egbert Dumond, Sheriff of Ulster county under the Crown, from 1771 to '73, from the first acted with the revolutionary party, and was a deputy in the Provincial Congress which met in May, 1775. In the same month an ordinance of the Convention appointed him Sheriff, which he held until 1781, and again from 1785 to '89. He was much engaged in public affairs during the revolution, and seems to have been greatly relied upon by the executive authority of these times.

Arthur Parks.—Member for the county in the 3d and 4th Provincial Congresses, and Major of Minute Men, and Senator from the middle district from 1777 to 1788   He appears to have been appointed Surrogate in 1785, but probably did not qualify, and in 1801 was chosen a member of the Constitutional Convention.   In Eager's *History of Orange County* it is said he died in Montgomery, Aug. 11th, 1806, in the 70th year of his age.

Col. Levi Pawling.—Levi Pawling of Marbletown was appointed Colonel of the Ulster County Militia, at the organization under the revolutionary government, his commission bearing date Oct. 25th, 1775. In July 1776, he is ordered into active service at the Highlands, and his regiment continued on duty there for several months.

Col Pawling possessed the confidence of the people, and was one of the three delegates to the Provincial Convention which met at the Exchange in New York, in April, 1775, and was also of the Congresses of 1776 and 1777. The Convention appointed him first judge of the county, May 8th, 1777, and this office he held during the remainder of his life. At the general election in 1777 he became a Senator, and in 1782 was again chosen — during his first term being a member of the Council of Appointment   He was the senior officer and commanded the handful of men who opposed the landing of the British at Esopus, on the 16th of October, 1777.   Col. Pawling died in 1782.   His son, Albert Pawling, was Brigade Major to Governor Clinton in the beginning of the war ; — afterwards removed to Troy, and a biography of him is given in Judge Woodworth's *Reminiscences* (p. 53).

John Nicholson, raised a company of men for the Continental army in July, 1775. Deputy in the first Provincial Congress, and a resident of New Windsor.

Moses Cantine, resided at Marbletown ; Member of the Assembly of 1800 ; was one of the Judges of Common Pleas. Died at Marbletown in July, 1827, aged 74.

Cornelius C. Schoonmaker.—This Mr. Schoonmaker, of Shawangunk, was Chairman of the County Committee at one time ; was chosen a member of Assembly nearly every year from 1777 to 1795. From 1791 to '93 represented the district in the second Congress of the United States and had been sent as a delegate to the Constitutional Convention of 1778. Mr. Schoonmaker had been a surveyor by profession, and occasionally tried his own real estate cases in the Supreme Court. He died at no great age in February or March, 1796. The Hon. Marius Schoonmaker of Kingston is his grandson.

Jacob Hoornbeck. — Appointed Lieutenant Colonel of Pawling's regiment, Oct. 25th, 1775. Most of the time during the early part of the revolution, chairman of the Rochester Committee of Safety, and in May,

1775, a deputy to the first Provincial Congress. He died of a camp fever, after a lingering illness, on the 10th of January, 1778, and was buried in the church-yard at Rochester. (*Hasbrouck MS. Diary*.)

SAMUEL BREWSTER.—Chairman of the precinct committee in 1777. Was a senator from the Middle District from 1805 to 1808,—resided at New Windsor.

MATTHEW REA.—A member of the 2d, 3d, and 4th Provincial Congresses, and also a member of Assembly from Ulster county, from 1777 to 1779. He resided in Shawangunk.

HENRY WISNER, JR.—Member of the 2d, 3d, and 4th Provincial Conventions; In 1785 was appointed Surrogate of Ulster county. In 1777-78 he represented Ulster in the Assembly, and after the severance of some towns from Ulster, again represented his district in 1788 and '89 ; I suppose that he was a son of Henry Wisner, of Goshen, one of the distinguished men of Orange during the Revolutionary period, but of whom this is not the place to speak particularly. Enger's *History of Orange County* gives very little information about the Wisners.

——

NOTE V.

COL. ABRAHAM HASBROUCK.

Abraham Hasbrouck, the son of Joseph and grandson of Abraham Hasbrouck, one of the twelve proprietors of the New Paltz patent, was born at Guilford near New Paltz village, Aug. 21st, 1707. June 11th, 1735, he removed to Kingston and lived in the house in East Front, at the head of Main Street, now known as Schryver's hotel. On the 5th of January, 1738, he married Catharine, daughter of Jacobus Bruyn, of Shawangunk.

In 1757, we find him Colonel of the Ulster county militia, and a letter from him to Lieut. Gov. Delancy, detailing an Indian attack upon the town of Rochester is in the *Doc. His.* (II. p. 764,)—was a member of the Colonial Assembly from 1739 to 1745, 1748 to 1750, and again from 1759 to 1768. Col Hasbrouck occupied a prominent position in the political history of his time, and took an active part in the movements of the patriots of the revolution. In Oct., 1775, he was appointed by the Provincial Congress Lieutenant Colonel of the regiment of militia commanded by Col. Johannes Snyder. Considerable difficulty in regard to rank arose among the officers of the several regiments, evidently increased by the appointment of George Clinton as Brigadier General of the district. The officers of the Northern regiment remonstrated with the Provincial Congress, and the correspondence has been printed with the Journal of that body (Vol. I, p. 153). In consequence of this difficulty, Colonel Hasbrouck declined to serve, and after some twenty years continuance in his position retired from military life. He was deputy to the Third Provincial Congress which met at White Plains, and after the revolution represented the county in the Assembly of 1781-82, but on account of his advancing years declined a re-election to that body.

Col Hasbrouck was a gentleman of considerable antiquarian taste and his collections relative to the early history of the county, it is said, were quite valuable, but unfortunately they were lost at the burning of his house in 1776. The only article of this sort preserved, was the family record which has been before quoted and from which some of these details are taken. After a life of usefulness and credit, he died Nov. 10th, 1791, and was buried, with military honors, at Kingston.

8

The other Colonel (Jonathan) Hasbrouck of this period was a younger brother of Abraham, and resided in the house commonly termed " Washington's Headquarters," at Newburgh.

———

Note VI.

COL. JONATHAN HASBROUCK.

Jonathan Hasbrouck was the younger son of Joseph Hasbrouck, of Guilford, in the precinct of New Paltz, Ulster county, where he was born about the year 1722. In May, 1751, he was married to Tryntje, (Catharine) daughter of Cornelius DuBois, and shortly after removed to Newburgh and there he continued to reside during the remainder of his life. This gentleman held various local offices, and his commission as Colonel of the Southern regiment of Ulster County militia is dated Oct. 25th, 1775. The regiment was often called out, but from the ill health of Col Hasbrouck was commanded much of the time by the Lieutenant Colonel, Johannes Hardenbergh, Jr. and it was under him at the time of Governor Clinton's forced march to succor Kingston in 1777. In the appendix may be found a return of the service performed by this regiment. Col. Hasbrouck enlarged the house at Newburgh, well known as "Washington's Head Quarters," and it remained in the possession of the family nearly a century, but it is now the property of the State and cared for by the trustees of the village of Newburgh. Lossing's *Field Book*, (II p. 99) has a good view of it. In consequence of continued ill health Col Hasbrouck resigned his military commission in 1778, and died July 31st, 1780. (*Hasbrouck MS. Diary,—Jour. Prov. Conv.*)

———

Note VII.

JACOBUS LEFFERTS.

Jacobus Lefferts, a New York Alderman, and a man of fortune, holding a large landed estate in Ulster county, and who was probably staying there to secure its possession, resided in the house (termed on *Knockston Point* in an advertisement I have seen), not far from the Saugerties road — near the residence of Cornelius Bruyn, Esq.,—and now owned by Peter J DuBois. His sympathies were undoubtedly with the Crown, and in a list of Tories in the *Clinton Papers* at Albany, he " has the King's protection." Mr. Lefferts married in April, 1772, Lucretia Brinckerhoff.

A letter from Gen. Jno. Morin Scott, in the same MSS., will illustrate the matter, as well as show that the leading men of the State were not always disposed to mete out even to Tories, the same measure Sir Henry Clinton and his plunderers were giving them.

" MARBLE TOWN, Novʳ 7ᵗʰ 1777.

" Dear Sir,

" At the request of Mr Leffertse I trouble you with his case. When General Warners Brigade passed thro' Kingston an Officer in his name took from Mr Leffertse his Coach Horses of Great Value, for the General's Use, tho' he offered the officer a good pair of Waggon Horses in their stead. Mr Leffertse se t his clerk after them, but could get only one of them back. The best of the two and one of the most valuable in the country is still detained and all he could get for it is a Receipt of which the inclosed is a copy. Such wanton liberty with mens property are not to be tolerated. We have suffered too much by abuses of the like kind committed by Troops of other States passing thro' this. We are contending in vain for our Liberty ag^t British Tyranny if we are to be subject to internal oppression. At least if General Warner wanted Horses he should have applied to some proper authority within this State for a supply. As General Warner may be in your way, I could wish, Sir, you would prevail on him to send Mr. Leffertse Horse back to him unhurt. For whatever his political character may be, on which I shall not take on me to decide, He and his property are under the protection of the Government nor is either of them to be taken from him by Military Force. I am

Sir,

With great respect
Your Excellency's
Most obedient servant
Jno. Morin Scott."

His Excellency Govr Clinton.

Note VIII.

CHARLES DEWITT.

After Governor Clinton the most prominent man of Ulster county, during the Revolution, was Charles DeWitt, of Greenkill, as he subscribed himself, a locality near Kingston. Before the separation from Great Britain he represented the county in the Colonial Assembly from 1768 to 1775, and as a member of the last legislative body which sat under the royal authority, was one of the nine resolute and patriotic men who voted to approve of the proceedings of the Continental Congress, then recently organized at Philadelphia. This and other rebellious symptoms soon induced Governor Tryon to dissolve the Assembly, and we next find him at the head of the County Committee of Safety, taking measures to secure the liberty which was now to be fought for in the open field. His leading position at once places him in the Provincial Convention of April 1775, and his name frequently occurs in the Journals of the subsequent Congresses, as well as in the Committee of Safety sitting in the recess of the larger bodies. He was appointed Colonel of a regiment of Minute Men, Dec 21st, 1775, but does not appear to have devoted his attention to the particular duties of his military command ; indeed this plan of raising a reliable force of this sort, was found somewhat impracticable and soon fell into neglect. On the appointment of the important committee of Congress " for detecting and defeating conspiracies, &c.," Col. DeWitt is placed upon it with William Duer, Zeph. Platt, Col. Van Courtlandt, John Jay, &c., and he continued to serve for a considerable time. When it was resolved to take the necessary steps to form a state government, the Convention elected Col. DeWitt a member of the committee to prepare a draft of the Constitution, and the one reported by them, was, after no great discussion, adopted, April 20, 1777, and under it the people passed through the revolutionary struggle, and came out a free and independent government

The arrest of Col DeWitt as an absconding recruit, by an officer of Snyder's regiment, arising evidently from some local jealousy, was made the subject of a "question of privilege," in the Convention ; the committee seemed determined to probe the matter to the bottom, and they examined all the parties charged with the offence, and finally compelled sundry persons to purge themselves of contempt into which the House voted them.

In 1784, he was chosen a delegate to the Continental Congress. After the close of the war the country had still need of his services, and from 1781 to 1785 he sat in the Assembly of the State. From a printed slip upon a portrait in possession of one of his descendants, Richard DeWitt, Esq., it would seem that he died April 27th, 1787. A photograph from this portrait, is in the Society's archives. His son, Charles G. DeWitt, edited the *Ulster Sentinel* for many years, represented the district in Congress, and was chargé d'affaires of the United States to one of the South American republics.

Note IX.

CHRISTOPHER TAPPEN.

Was born at Kingston in June, 1742, and descended from one of the early settlers of Esopus. He must have been a surveyor by profession, but acted for many years as deputy to his brother-in-law, George Clinton, who held the Ulster County Clerkship for the unprecedented period of sixty years, viz: 1752 to 1812. While he was Governor of the State, and even when he became Vice President of the United States. We find Tappen's name constantly connected with Kingston, whether in the Trustees' records or the doings of the authorities of the venerable church at Esopus, or as a civil magistrate. Of course such a man, in such a locality, would be found upon the popular side in the struggle for independence, and he soon appears in the deliberations of the County Committee, and represented Ulster in the 1st, 3d, and 4th Provincial Congresses, and his prominence there placed him often in the Council of Safety. On the organization of the regiments of minute-men in Dec. 1775, he is appointed a Major, but probably did not see much active duty, his abilities being more valued in the civil service of the country. Major Tappen was a member of the secret committee for obstructing the navigation of the Hudson, in July, 1776, and had previously, in conjunction with James Clinton, prepared a plan for fortifying the Highlands. After the Revolution, Major Tappen sat in the Assembly in 1788, 1789 and 1790, and was elected Senator from the Middle District in 1797. He is named in the act creating the first Board of Regents of the University in 1784. After the death of Governor Clinton, in 1812, he was appointed Clerk of the county, and thus the office continued in the family until 1821, when the weight of years, no doubt, induced Major Tappen to resign it. He died August 3d, 1826, and was buried at Kingston. A long obituary notice by his son, John J. Tappen, editor of the *Plebian*, is in the paper of the 9th of August, 1826.

DOCUMENTS.

No. I.

Letter from Commodore Hotham to the Viscount Howe.

Preston off Peeks Kilncreek
15. Octr 1777.

My Lord,

Since I had the honour to write to you by the Apollo, not any thing material has happened here; but Sir Henry Clinton having occasion to write to the Commander in Chief, I take the same opportunity to acquaint your lordship, that the Number of men which would be necessary for the Defence of the more extensive Garrison of Fort Montgomery, has induced Sir Henry to destroy it, & to add some works to that of Fort Clinton which commanding the first, effectually removes all apprehension from thence, and reduces the Force necessary to maintain it to about 800 men. This has enabled him to send a Detachment of about 1600 men up the North River under General Vaughan; Sir James Wallace who has already explored the River as high as Pakepsy, directs the Naval Part consisting of the Gallies & small vessels as before; and Captⁿ Stanhope under him commands the Detachment of Flat Boats appointed for the occasion.

They sailed yesterday, & are now above the Chevaux de frize off Pollepus Island, where I have placed the Mercury to secure that Passage against their return, & the Cerberus being reported to me as only fit for River service takes her station off Stoney Point to scour that neck, & to give her assistance at the same time to the Camp at Verplanks.

The Tartar flanks approaches to Fort Clinton, & the Preston lies between the two, within signals of either.

The principal object of the move up the River is to facilitate the motions (whatever they may be) of the Northern Army, and by the alarm which it will occasion to cause a Diversion in their Favour.

The Unicorn was to sail to-day with a Convoy of victuallers for Rhode Island. The Galatea's rudder was dropping off and has been obliged to be unhung & the Braces Standing as well as Running Rigging mostly condemned by Survey.

I have the honour to be
My Lord,
Your Lordships most obedient
humble Servant

(*Admiralty, American Depmt.*) W. HOTHAM.

No. II.

Letter from Commodore Hotham to the Viscount Howe.

St Albans New York. 21st Octr 1777

My Lord,

My Letters of the 15th instant which you will herewith receive were Intended to have been sent by the Bristol, who is stopped to proceed with the Convoy directed by your Lordships Letter of the 10th . In consequence of it I have left the command up the North River with Captain Symonds until the return of General Vaughan when it is intended to evacuate every thing there, as Sir Henry Clinton for the defence of this place will now stand in need of every man left under his command.

The proceedings of the second expedition up the River your Lordship will see by the inclosed Copy of a Letter from Sir James Wallace, & one also to Sir Henry Clinton from General Vaughan The wind having hung to the Southward ever since, has prevented our hearing any thing farther from them : but as it last night shifted & now blows strong from the North West, it is reasonable to think we shall have them down, the object of their going up the River seeming to be now over, without giving credit to the whole of what we hear respecting General Burgoyne's army. The two Battalions of Anspach were embarked before Sir Henry Clinton and I left Verplanks Point and with the wind may be hourly expected down. The 17th Dragoons with the Convalescents, Recruits, Chasseurs & Artillery will be embarked without loss of time, and shall proceed (as they are ready) in separate convoys, which from the experience I have had of large ones, I consider as the securest and most expeditions way for them to join you. The 7th 26th & 63d Regiments are embarked with General Vaughan

Some of the horse ships are got up to York and the rest of the Thames's Convoy are with her within the Hook, so that we shall not be in any want of Transports for the embarkation, nor shall expedition be less wanting to forward it. This gives me an opportunity of doing the justice I owe to Lieutenant Tonkin the Agent whose Assiduity and Resources are felt upon every occasion where his services are called for.

I have the honour to transmit you this despatch by Capt Kennedy who is charged with Sir Henry Clinton's to Sir William Howe by an armed vessel of Colonel Shiriffs the Haerlem having been necessarily employed up the River. I have the honor to be

My Lord
Your most obedient
humble servt.

(*Admiralty, American Deptmt.*)　　　　　W. HOTHAM.

No. III.

Gen. James Clinton to Governor Clinton.

Little Britain Octobr 18. 1777

Dr Brother.

Yours of yesterdays date I have just Received. I am sorry for the loss of Kingston &c

Five of the Enemys Shipping Returned Down the River Last night without doing any damage, except firing some cannon and small arms at our men and wounding one of ours on Board of a Ferry Boat.

Inclosed I send you two Letters one from Gen. Dickeson and the other from Gen. Winds.——the latter I have answered by ordering him here as by your former Letter.

I have wrote to Gen. Putnam for a Reinforcement this Day and Expect Gen. Winds will be ordered to remain here.

I have ordered Capt Bellknap to move your slay and what Forage he can from the River.

I am yours affectionately,
JAMES CLINTON, B Genl

P. S. Gen. Parsons remains at Peekskill with about 2000. Colonels Humphreys, & Brinkerhoof Regiments of Militia Left at Fish-Kill, Colonel Platt with about 150 at Poughkeepsie.

To His Excellency Govr Clinton.

No. IV.

Morning Report of the Main Guard of Gov. Clinton's Army, Oct. 18. 1777.

HURLEY, Oct. 18, 1777.

A morning report of the Main Guard consisting of,

Parole.	Capt.	Sub'n.	Serg't.	Corp'l.	Privates.	Centries by Day, 10.
Counter Sign, Herd.	1	2	3	3	35	Centries by Night, 7.

Visited the Centinels frequently, found them alert, on their posts. No Grand Rounds. Nothing material happened.

The names of the Prisoners confined and their names,

Isaac Van Vleck, taken up as a Spy.

Daniel Taylor, taken up as a Spy.

Jonathan Van Waggoner, confined for going over to Long Island to the Enemy and Returning to Ulster County.

Wm Mohany Confined for saying the Rebels were retreating before Genl Burgoyne & that he hoped the Rebels would be beat.

James Henter, Molato Confined for going into New York, with wood & coming out again & being found with Tories.

Thomas Porter for Speaking disrespectfully of our General and Under Officers that Commanded at Fort Montgomery and for saying that if it had been Commanded by British Officers it would not have been given up.

Mathew McKenney of Capt Glaspyes Comp^y of Col. Hasbroucks Reg^t. Militia confined by Lieu^t Hunter, for having Spoken Treason against the State.

Jeremiah Fitzgerald, Stephen Anderson & Benjⁿ Andrews, Confined by Major Miffitt for plundering of Leather from the House of Theophilus Carwin, which was found in the Custody and allso for Refusing to Stop when ordered by the Cent^l. Bart Miller Confined by Ensⁿ Mumford, for being an Enemy to his Country and saying that he was a friend to George the third King of Great Britain.

John Comfort
Benjⁿ Comfort
Jon^a Harris
John St Clair   Charged with being Enemies to the States
Godfrey Kuiver   & being found In Arms against the States
Maliaga Seager   Confined by Lt Col^o Hardenbergh
John Poof
Aaron Cruver
Yose Henry Tiso

John Stump of Capt Stewarts Comp^y Col^o Dubois's Reg^t.

John Hole a Tory, Confined for being a guide to a party of Col^o Saml B. Webb thinking they were British Regulars and piloting from his own house

Jacob Lowes who is said was raising a Comp^y for the British service

Daniel Wakeman Capt Johnstons Comp^y of Militia, Col^o Hasbrooks Reg^t Confined for Disobedience of orders, and Refusing to march when Legally warned at the late alarm, Confined by John Hardenbergh Lieu^t Col^o of said Reg^t. (Regimental).

Henry Horrill of Col^o Pawling's Reg^t Militia Confined for disaffection & Speaking Treasonable against the States of North America, Confined by Lieu^t Col^o Johannis Hardenbergh.

Samuel Townsend Nathaniel Waters Robert Hess	All of Col^o Pawlings Reg^t Militia, Confined by Daniel Freer Ensign, for neglect of Duty & Disobedience of Orders. (Regimental)
John Christis Henry Tise Daniel Cogal Henry Hurl John Cassell	All Confined by Col^o Hardenbergh of Disobedience of Orders and Disaffection to the States.

Abraham Brinkerhoff by Major Winecup—Released—

JOHN ELLIS,
Officer of the Guard.

No. V.

Governor Clinton to Gen. Putnam.

Hurley, Oct 20. 1777

Sir,

I have this moment received your letter of this Date, with the letters you mention—concerning them I have only to congratulate you on the fortunate event by which the present purposes of the Enemy are defeated.

With respect to the Galley—she is sunk about two miles from the landing place There will be some difficulty in raising the cannon Especially the 32 p^{dr} — for which we have no carriage on this side However if you can send me a traveling carriage and ammunition I will endeavor to bring her on shore—

I very much approve of your intention to annoy the enemy's fleet & shall cheerfully co-operate with you & as General Gates is arrived in Albany. The cannon may soon be procured,--What think you of attempting Fort Montgomery ?—by General Parsons & the Troops from Jersey. GEORGE CLINTON.

To the Hon^b Major General Putnam, Red Hook.

No. VI.

Report of the " Officer of the Day " of the Army at Hurley.

Hurley Town Octob^r 20, 1777
Head Quarters

A Morning Report of the Officer of the day, who visited the Guards & Pickets.

Coll. Webbs Pickquets, Coll. Dubois and Coll. Sutherland all sufficient, Coll. Hasbroucks and Ellisons Deficient of Arms and Ammunition—

By Report of Officer of the Main Guard countersign *N York.* The

Centinels being frequently visited, found alert on their Posts, and the Guard consisting of,

Capt.	Lieut's.	Serg'ts.	Corp'ls.	Privates.	Total,	Centinels	
						by Day	by Night
1	2	3	3	44	50	12	12

The number of Prisoners confined in the Main Guard 27 with the Crimes given, and 9 without Crimes,

Given under my hand,
Joh⁹ HARDENBERGH Col.

P. S. The Gnard at Kingston deficient of Light Horse & Guides.

No. VII.

A Report of the Guard at Kingston, 20th October, 1777.

Perole Boston. C. New York.

	Capt.	Lieut.	Serg't.	Corp'l.	Privates.	Countersign by Day.	Do by Night.
Detail of Guard.	1	3	4	4	65	6	10

JOHN MINTHORN Officer
of the Guard

Nothing strange }
since Guard Mounting. }

	Lieut.	Serg't.	Corp'l.	Privates.
A Detail of Piequet Guard.	1	1	1	13

Patrolling parties Kept out all Night.

No. VIII.

Col. Hasbrouck's Reg't. of Militia—Services 1776 to 1778.

A return of the Extraordinary Services Lately performed by Collo. Hasbrouck's Regiment of Militia since the 18th day of December, 1776, from Time to Time, the Number of Men in Service, on what particular Service, & what Term of Time.

What particular Service has been performed.	No. of Men.	What Term of Time.
First, At the Alarm December 12, 1776 at Ramapaugh,	300	27 days.
2d At Ramapaugh from 7th January, 2 & 1777,..	100	14 do
3d Under Col. Pawling from 2 &c of Jany 1777 till last of April 1777, at Ramapaugh, ...	200	40 do
4th Under Colo Snyder at Fort Montgomery 4 months,............................	150	120 do
5th Under Colo Ellison at Fort Montgomery 3 months, ...	130	90 do
6th At the Alarm in March 1777, when the Stores was destroyed at Peekskill,........	200	4 do
7th At the Alarm at Fort Montgomery in July 1777, ...	460	8 do
6th At the Alarm at Fort Montgomery in Augt 1777, ...	500	8 do
9th At the Alarm at Fort Montgomery in Sept 1777, ...	400	8 do
10th At Fort Constitution the 1st October 1777, under the Command of Majr Dubois,....	200	10 do
11th The Alarm at the burning of Esopus in Octr 1777, ...	460	30 do
12tb, the Six weeks Service at Nicholas's Point in Novr 1777, under the Command of Colo Heathorn, ...	120	45 do
13tb At the West Point in March & Ap. 1778, under Mr Wisner, ...	420	8 do

Given under my hand this 18th day of June, 1778.

Errors Excepted

Jon's HARDENBERGH,

Lt Colo

To his Excellency
George Clinton Esqr

———

No. IX.

Address of the Committee of Kingston to Governor Clinton respecting their desire of rebuilding the village. 9th Feby 1778.

To his Excellency George Clinton Esqr Governor and Commander-in-Chief of the State of New York.

The Humble Address of the Committee of Safety & Observation of the town of Kingston,

Humbly make known,

That whereas a Dispute is raised Between America and the King of Great Britain touching & Concerning Taxation America held such Taxation unjust & illegal and unwarrantable by the Constitution of Britain America soon entered upon & into measures to prevent such illegal tax Kingston unitedly did join and seconded the measures to prevent the Expected oppression by their early embarking in the cause of Liberty and their persevering & continued Exertions in support thereof have undoubtedly incurred the bitterest resentment of the Enemy to Vent such resentment & Expedition up the North river was determined upon and the destruction of Kingston thereby effected and completed to the great loss & Damage of the Inhabitants Sir many of the Sufferers wou'd fain build are Discouraged by means of the enormous prizes of things

& Labour the unhappy Sufferers have always supported the cause with proper spirit have always submitted to the present Government cheerfully turned out their Number of men on all Detachments and those ordered to be raised to Reinforce the Army and always acted with spirit and Resolution however the situation circumstances & Difficulties the Committee thinks it there indispensible Duty to address your Excellency in behalf of the sufferers of Kingston that your Excellency therefore will be pleased to make use of your Interest in Devising means whereby the poor Sufferers may obtain Relief, their Spirit to Rebuild the town is good but their abilities Weak Assistance for that purpose would be Exceedingly agreeable, and mightily revive the present Dejection of many of the poor Sufferers the committee may it please your Excellency concludes by praying that your Excellency will use all your Influence & Interest to obtain Relief for the poor Sufferers of Kingston

By order of the Committee

ANDRIES DEWITT JUN^r Ch.

No. X.

Gov. Clinton's reply to the address of the Committee of Kingston in regard to rebuilding the town

Poughkeepsie 17th Feby 1778

Sir,

I have received the Address of the Committee of Kingston dated the 9th inst respecting the Distresses of the Inhabitants of Kingston & the aid required to enable them to rebuild the Town. You may rest assured Gentlemen that whatever may be in my power to render them shall not be witheld but most cheerfully afforded I have already suggested to sundry members of the Legislature the Propriety of rebuilding the Court House and Goal at public Expense & have Reason to hope it will be done I have likewise mentioned the propriety of Exempting such Number of Artificers as shall be necessary, from Military Drafts & Duty providing they agree to work at rebuilding the town for Reasonable wages, which likewise I hope I shall be enabled to do.

As to Freer I think no Publick Injury can arise from his continuing at home at Present, in the Mean Time I will lay his case before the commissioners for detecting conspiracies, to be appointed in pursuance of a late act of the Legislature, who I have no doubt will deal with him according to Justice in such Manner as will conduce most the Public Safety & Peace.   I am with due Respect

Your most obed^t serv^t

GEO. CLINTON.

No. XI.

A Return of Col^l Levi Pawling's Regiment of Militia. Dated in Marbletown, this 17th Day of Feby 1776.

The Names of the Captains Commanding the Companies.	Colonel.	Lieut Coll.	Majors.	Captains.	Lieutenants.	Ensigns.	Sergeants.	Corporals.	Drummers & Fifers.	Privates.
Field Officers,	1	..	2	..	..	..	..	..	....	....
Captain Jacob Hasbrouck,	..	..	..	1	2	1	4	4	1	41
Capt Frederick Schoonmaker,	..	..	..	1	2	1	4	4	1	62
Capt Andries Bevier,	..	..	..	1	2	1	3	4	1	51
Capt Peleg Ransom,	..	..	..	1	1	1	4	4	1	46
Capt Jocham Schoonmaker,	..	..	..	1	2	1	4	4	1	49
Capt John A. Hardenbergh,	..	..	..	1	1	1	3	3	....	43
Capt John Hasbrouck,	..	..	..	1	1	1	4	4	....	40
Capt Charles W. Brodhead,	..	..	..	1	2	1	3	2	1	39
Capt Benjamin Kortreght,	..	..	..	1	2	1	4	4	1	52
	1	..	2	9	15	9	33	33	7	423

LEVI PAWLING, Col^{o.}

No. XII.

Ulster County Militia Officers.

The following list is from the *Jour. of the Prov. Conv.*, (II. p. 134) :

" A list of field officers for the county of Ulster, viz : Col. Johannes Hardenburgh, Lieut. Col. Abraham Hasbrouck, Maj. Johannes Snyder, Maj. Jonathan Elmendorf, Adj't Petrus I. Elmendorf, Quarter-Master Abraham A. Hasbrouck.

Col. James Clinton, Lieut. Col. James Claughry, Major Jacob Newkerk, Major Moses Phillips, Adj't George Denniston, Quarter-Master Alexander Trimble ; commissions dated 25th Oct., 1775.

Col. Levi Pawling, Lieut. Col. Jacob Hornbeck, Maj. Johannes Cantine, Maj. Joseph Hasbrouck, Adj't David Bevier, Quarter-Master Jacobus Bruyn, Jr. ; commissions dated 25th Oct., 1775.

Col. Jonathan Hasbrouck, Lieut. Col. Johannes Hardenbergh, Jr , Maj. Johannes Jansen, Jr., Maj. Lewis DuBois, Adj't. Abraham Schoonmaker, Quarter-Master Isaac Belknap ; commissions dated 25th Oct., 1775.

INDEX.

www.ingramcontent.com/pod-product-compliance
Lightning Source LLC
Chambersburg PA
CBHW020233090426
42735CB00010B/1677